D1265135

Memories of the American Frontier: Theodore Roosevelt

History has been gracious to the presidents who watch the stars from near the summit on Mount Rushmore in Dakota Country. George Washington is here, and Thomas Jefferson, and Abraham Lincoln.

Another, Theodore Roosevelt, is also appropriately here, for, in addition to his accomplishments as the youngest of this group, he knew firsthand the majesty of this land, the rough virtues and the rugged integrity of its people; its stalwart democracy where every man stood for what he was and could show himself to be.

A man of inspired idealism, Theodore Roosevelt strove to make his dreams of the future come true, and later in life he kindled the people of America with the fire of enthusiasm and a vision of greatness that would lead an adolescent nation into the 20th century. But not all of Roosevelt's ideals were founded in the classrooms of Harvard, or in the political chambers of New York. The wilderness helped forge his values, tested his character, restored the strength he had lost through tragedy, and gave him stamina and resolution.

The stories you are about to read were written by a young Theodore Roosevelt who, shortly after losing both his wife and mother within hours of each other on the same day in

1884, gave up the life of a promising New York politician. He, like other pioneers of his day, headed West, and what began as a brief diversion on life's road turned out to be a tempering episode in the maturation of a future leader of ninety million Americans.

Roosevelt once wrote, "I never would have been President if it had not been for my experience in North Dakota." While he sometimes regarded his life on the range as an "idyllic interlude," he contended that the "romance of my life began there." Here he had a place to practice the "strenuous life." Here he had time to get to know people, and he admired them greatly. Here he found the inspiration that would later encourage him to organize the Rough Riders, bringing him fame during the Spanish-American War in 1898, furthering his progress on the road to the Presidency in 1901.

The adventure began in the fall of 1883, when Roosevelt undertook his first hunting expedition to the Bad Lands. He utilized the guide services of a cowboy by the name of Joe Ferris. Ferris took Roosevelt to the Chimney Butte, or Maltese Cross Ranch, operated by Joe's brother, Sylvane, and his partner, William J. Merrifield. The hunt went on as planned, but a good deal of conversation also took place. They talked about the prospects of the cattle industry on the northern plains. By the time the expedition ended, Roosevelt had made the decision to invest in the ranching business, and before returning to New York, he purchased the Maltese Cross Ranch.

By the next summer, he acquired 1,000 head of cattle. He selected a site for a second ranch on the Little Missouri River, the Elkhorn Ranch, which was completed in the early summer of 1885. And within the following year, Roosevelt's cattle operations reached a peak of between 3,000 and 5,000 head. Wearing the attire of a cowhand, he often spent 14 to 16 hours a day in the saddle. He tended cattle. He hunted buffalo and other game. He even helped capture a band of outlaws. The austere, hard life helped him forget his sorrow.

In addition to his chores as a ranchman, Roosevelt turned to writing. At Maltese Cross, he completed *Hunting Trips of a Ranchman* (1885); at Elkhorn, he wrote most of his *Life of Thomas Hart Benton* (1886). He also served as president of the Little Missouri Stockmen's Association. Life in the Bad Lands began to look very good indeed.

However, in the winter of 1886-1887, fate intervened in what otherwise might have encouraged Roosevelt to remain to the end of the era. Many southern plains cattlemen, plagued by drought and brush fires, had moved their herds northward during the previous summer into the already overstocked forage areas in the Dakotas. When winter arrived with heavy snow, partial thawing and freezing, crusting the ground with ice, the weakened cattle froze, starved or fell prey to predators. Some estimated the loss as high as seventy-five percent. Roosevelt lost more than half his herd, and from then on he was inclined to devote more of his time to his family and political career back in New York. Even though he visited the Bad Lands less frequently, his cattle ranching efforts continued but with only limited success. In 1898 he sold out to Sylvane Ferris.

Despite what some characterize as his failure as a rancher, Roosevelt's love of the West endured. He idealized his frontier experiences in his multivolume *The Winning of the West* (1889-1896). He wrote numerous other books and a series of stories about ranching published in *Century Magazine*.

This limited edition, designed by Bradbury Thompson, is liberally illustrated with wood engraving reproductions of drawings by Frederic Remington, a friend of Theodore Roosevelt, and America's most famous illustrator of life in the wild West. It is the twentieth in the Westvaco series and continues the tradition of other volumes in the collection.

Memories of the American Frontier is notable in a number of ways. As always, Thompson has used materials available from the author's time, beginning with Caslon Old Face which is the same type used in Roosevelt's *The Wilderness Hunter,* published in 1891. The use of Caslon type was even then a revival of its previous wide usage in the 18th century. It should be mentioned however that this edition is set by computer-programmed phototypography.

The text is set flush left, ragged right in a modern but informal style as TR wrote it—more intimate, more as he might have prepared his first draft. This design of the printed page embodies the typographer's art at its finest, facilitating readability and yet giving a nice quality of the time in harmony with the rugged outdoor nature of the subject itself. To bring them to life, the conversational sections with frontier dialect are set in phrases, line by line, just as they might be spoken. This innovative typographic concept was originally used in our 1974 edition of *Daisy Miller* by Henry James.

For illustrations, Thompson used the reproductions of drawings by Remington that appeared originally in *Century Magazine* shortly before being published in book form in collaboration with Roosevelt.

Conveying the stark, seemingly endless grandeur of the prairie is the designer's genius in blending color and texture, such as the bit of green and predominant tan of the buckram cover, the slip case, and the end papers. The symbolic saddle and other decorative illustrations, are all from original Roosevelt books from which the text was adapted.

Also, stamped into the front cover is TR's own cattle brand, which may appear to be both a Maltese cross or four Ts, secured after considerable research and authentication. The motif on the end papers also carries a similar design of crosses. It is a blanket woven by Indians during the time portrayed in our book.

The author's preface is followed by his signature, and the title page with its exceptional poetic excerpt, written by

Roosevelt, faces one of Remington's works. The small decorative drawings, which adorn the pages used to divide parts of the book, are from Roosevelt's *The Wilderness Hunter,* and although they carry the initials F and two Rs back to back, we believe them not to be the work of Frederic Remington.

Each of the chapters begins with a two-page frontispiece. Each drawing is backed up by another, complementing the appearance of the finely-textured, uncoated book paper of natural shade.

Theodore Roosevelt once said:"Keep your eyes on the stars, but remember to keep your feet on the ground."

The delightful reading in this twentieth Westvaco limited edition will give you some insight into the practical philosophy of the twenty-sixth President of the United States, an early advocate of conservation; a practical adherent of multiple use of the land for commerce and industry, recreation and wildlife management; a proponent of genuine stewardship of the land to assure its ability to produce abundantly for generations to come.

This Edition is Published by Westvaco, Christmas 1977

For a number of years much of my life was spent
either in the wilderness or on the borders of the
settled country—if, indeed, "settled" is a term that
can rightly be applied to the vast, scantily peopled
regions where cattle-ranching is the only regular
industry. During this time I hunted much, among
the mountains and on the plains, both as a pastime
and to procure hides, meat, and robes for use on the
ranch; and it was my good luck to kill all the
various kinds of large game that can properly be
considered to belong to temperate North America.

In hunting, the finding and killing of the game
is after all but a part of the whole. The free, self-
reliant, adventurous life, with its rugged and
stalwart democracy; the wild surroundings, the
grand beauty of the scenery, the chance to study the
ways and habits of the woodland creatures—all these
unite to give to the career of the wilderness hunter
its peculiar charm. The chase is among the best of
all national pastimes; it cultivates that vigorous

manliness for the lack of which in a nation, as in an individual, the possession of no other qualities can possibly atone.

No one, but he who has partaken thereof, can understand the keen delight of hunting in lonely lands. For him is the joy of the horse well ridden and the rifle well held; for him the long days of toil and hardship, resolutely endured, and crowned at the end with triumph. In after years there shall come forever to his mind the memory of endless prairies shimmering in the bright sun; of vast snow-clad wastes lying desolate under gray skies; of the melancholy marshes; of the rush of mighty rivers; of the breath of the evergreen forest in summer; of the crooning of ice-armored pines at the touch of the winds of winter; of cataracts roaring between hoary mountain masses; of all the innumerable sights and sounds of the wilderness; of its immensity and mystery; and of the silences that brood in its still depths.

Theodore Roosevelt
Sagamore Hill
June, 1893

Contents

Memories of the American Frontier

Ranching in the Bad Lands

Cruising for Stock

The Round-Up

I
Ranching
in the Bad Lands

The great middle plains of the United States, parts
of which are still scantily peopled by men of
Mexican parentage, while other parts have been
but recently won from the warlike tribes of Horse
Indians, now form a broad pastoral belt, stretching
in a north and south line from British America to
the Rio Grande. Throughout this great belt of
grazing land almost the only industry is stock-
raising, which is here engaged in on a really
gigantic scale; and it is already nearly covered with
the ranches of the stockmen, except on those
isolated tracts (often themselves of great extent)
from which the red men look hopelessly and
sullenly out upon their old hunting-grounds, now
roamed over by the countless herds of long-horned
cattle. The northern portion of this belt is that
which has been most lately thrown open to
the whites; and it is with this part only that we
have to do.

The northern cattle plains occupy the basin of the
Upper Missouri; that is, they occupy all of the land

drained by the tributaries of that river, and by the river itself, before it takes its long trend to the southeast. They stretch from the rich wheat farms of Central Dakota to the Rocky Mountains, and southward to the Black Hills and the Big Horn chain, thus including all of Montana, Northern Wyoming, and extreme Western Dakota. The character of this rolling, broken, plains country is everywhere much the same. It is a high, nearly treeless region, of light rainfall, crossed by streams which are sometimes rapid torrents and sometimes merely strings of shallow pools. In places it stretches out into deserts of alkali and sage brush, or into nearly level prairies of short grass, extending for many miles without a break; elsewhere there are rolling hills, sometimes of considerable height; and in other places the ground is rent and broken into the most fantastic shapes, partly by volcanic action and partly by the action of water in a dry climate. These latter portions form the famous Bad Lands. Cotton-wood trees fringe the streams or stand in groves on the alluvial bottoms of the rivers; and some of the steep hills and canyon sides are clad with pines or stunted cedars. In the early spring, when the young blades first sprout, the land looks green and bright; but during the rest of the year there is no such appearance of freshness, for the short bunch grass is almost brown, and the gray-green sage bush, bitter and withered-looking, abounds everywhere, and gives a peculiarly barren aspect to the landscape.

It is but little over half a dozen years since these lands were won from the Indians. They were their only remaining great hunting-grounds, and towards the end of the last decade all of the northern plains tribes went on the war-path in a final desperate effort to preserve them. After bloody fighting and protracted campaigns they were defeated, and the country thrown open to the whites, while the building of the Northern Pacific Railroad gave immigration an immense impetus. There were great quantities of game, especially buffalo, and the hunters who thronged in to pursue the huge herds of the latter were the rough forerunners of civilization. No longer dreading the Indians, and having the railway on which to transport the robes, they followed the buffalo in season and out, until in 1883 the herds were practically destroyed. But meanwhile the cattle-men formed the vanguard of the white settlers. Already the hardy southern stockmen had pressed up with their wild-looking herds to the very border of the dangerous land, and even into it, trusting to luck and their own prowess for their safety; and the instant the danger was even partially removed, their cattle swarmed northward along the streams. Some Eastern men, seeing the extent of the grazing country, brought stock out by the railroad, and the short-horned beasts became almost as plenty as the wilder-looking southern steers. At the present time, indeed, the cattle of these northern ranges show more short-horn than long-horn blood.

Cattle-raising on the plains, as now carried on, started in Texas, where the Americans had learned it from the Mexicans whom they dispossessed.

It has only become a prominent feature of Western life during the last score of years. When the Civil War was raging, there were hundreds of thousands of bony, half wild steers and cows in Texas, whose value had hitherto been very slight; but toward the middle of the struggle they became a most important source of food supply to both armies, and when the war had ended, the profits of the business were widely known and many men had gone into it. At first the stock-raising was all done in Texas, and the beef-steers, when ready for sale, were annually driven north along what became a regular cattle trail. Soon the men of Kansas and Colorado began to start ranches, and Texans who were getting crowded out moved their herds north into these lands, and afterward into Wyoming. Large herds of yearling steers also were, and still are, driven from the breeding ranches of the south to some northern range, there to be fattened for three years before selling. The cattle trail led through great wastes, and the scores of armed cowboys who, under one or two foremen, accompanied each herd, had often to do battle with bands of hostile Indians; but this danger is now a thing of the past, as, indeed, will soon be the case with the cattle trail itself, for year by year the grangers press steadily westward into it, and when they have once settled in a place, will not permit the cattle to be driven across it.

In the northern country the ranches vary greatly in size; on some there may be but a few hundred head, on others ten times as many thousand. The land is still in great part unsurveyed, and is hardly anywhere fenced in, the cattle roaming over it at will. The small ranches are often quite close to one another, say within a couple of miles; but the home ranch of a big outfit will not have another building within ten or twenty miles of it, or, indeed, if the country is dry, not within fifty. The ranchhouse may be only a mud dugout, or a "shack" made of logs stuck upright into the ground; more often it is a fair-sized, well-made building of hewn logs, divided into several rooms. Around it are grouped the other buildings—log-stables, cow-sheds, and hay-ricks, an out-house in which to store things, and on large ranches another house in which the cowboys sleep. The strongly made, circular horse-corral, with a snubbing-post in the middle, stands close by; the larger cow-corral, in which the stock is branded, may be some distance off. A small patch of ground is usually enclosed as a vegetable garden, and a very large one, with water in it, as a pasture to be used only in special cases. All the work is done on horseback, and the quantity of ponies is thus of necessity very great, some of the large outfits numbering them by hundreds; on my own ranch there are eighty. Most of them are small, wiry beasts, not very speedy, but with good bottom, and able to pick up a living under the most adverse circumstances. There are usually a few large, fine horses kept for the special use of the ranchman or foremen. The best are those from Oregon; most of them come from Texas, and many are bought from the Indians. They are broken in a very rough manner, and many are in consequence vicious brutes, with the detestable habit of bucking. Of this habit I have a perfect dread, and,

if I can help it, never get on a confirmed bucker.
The horse puts his head down between his fore-
feet, arches his back, and with stiff legs gives a
succession of jarring jumps, often "changing ends"
as he does so. Even if a man can keep his seat, the
performance gives him about as uncomfortable a
shaking up as can be imagined.

The cattle rove free over the hills and prairies,
picking up their own living even in winter, all the
animals of each herd having certain distinctive
brands on them. But little attempt is made to keep
them within definite bounds, and they wander
whither they wish, except that the ranchmen
generally combine to keep some of their cowboys
riding lines to prevent them straying away
altogether. The missing ones are generally
recovered in the annual round-ups, when the calves
are branded. These round-ups, in which many
outfits join together, and which cover hundreds of
miles of territory, are the busiest period of the year
for the stockmen, who then, with their cowboys,
work from morning till night. In winter little is
done except a certain amount of line riding.

The cowboys form a class by themselves, and are
now quite as typical representatives of the wilder
side of Western life, as were a few years ago the
skin-clad hunters and trappers. They are mostly of
native birth, and although there are among them
wild spirits from every land, yet the latter soon
become undistinguishable from their American
companions, for these plainsmen are far from

being so heterogeneous a people as is commonly supposed. On the contrary, all have a certain curious similarity to each other; existence in the west seems to put the same stamp upon each and every one of them. Sinewy, hardy, self-reliant, their life forces them to be both daring and adventurous, and the passing over their heads of a few years leaves printed on their faces certain lines which tell of dangers quietly fronted and hardships uncomplainingly endured. They are far from being as lawless as they are described; though they sometimes cut queer antics when, after many months of lonely life, they come into a frontier town in which drinking and gambling are the only recognized forms of amusement, and where pleasure and vice are considered synonymous terms. On the round-ups, or when a number get together, there is much boisterous, often foul-mouthed mirth; but they are rather silent, self-contained men when with strangers, and are frank and hospitable to a degree. The Texans are perhaps the best at the actual cowboy work. They are absolutely fearless riders and understand well the habits of the half wild cattle, being unequalled in those most trying times when, for instance, the cattle are stampeded by a thunderstorm at night, while in the use of the rope they are only excelled by the Mexicans. On the other hand, they are prone to drink, and when drunk, to shoot. Many Kansans, and others from the northern States, have also taken up the life of late years, and though these scarcely reach, in point of skill and dash, the standard of the southerners, who may be said to be born in the saddle, yet they are to the full as resolute and even more trustworthy. My own foremen were originally eastern backwoodsmen.

The cowboy's dress is both picturesque and serviceable, and, like many of the terms of his pursuit, is partly of Hispano-Mexican origin. It consists of a broad felt hat, a flannel shirt, with a bright silk handkerchief loosely knotted round the neck, trousers tucked into high-heeled boots, and a pair of leather "shaps" (chaperajos) or heavy riding overalls. Great spurs and a large-calibre revolver complete the costume. For horse gear there is a cruel curb bit, and a very strong, heavy saddle with high pommel and cantle. This saddle seems needlessly weighty, but the work is so rough as to make strength the first requisite. A small pack is usually carried behind it; also saddle pockets, or small saddle-bags; and there are leather strings wherewith to fasten the loops of the raw-hide lariat. The pommel has to be stout, as one end of the lariat is twisted round it when work is to be done, and the strain upon it is tremendous when a vigorous steer has been roped, or when, as is often the case, a wagon gets stuck and the team has to be helped out by one of the riders hauling from the saddle. A ranchman or foreman dresses precisely like the cowboys, except that the materials are finer, the saddle leather being handsomely carved, the spurs, bit, and revolver silver-mounted, the shaps of seal-skin, etc. The revolver was formerly a necessity, to protect the owner from Indians and other human foes; this is still the case in a few places, but, as a rule, it is now carried merely from habit, or to kill rattlesnakes, or on the chance of falling in with a wolf or coyote, while not unfrequently it is used to add game to the cowboy's not too varied bill of fare.

A cowboy is always a good and bold rider, but his seat in the saddle is not at all like that of one of our eastern or southern fox-hunters. The stirrups are so long that the man stands almost erect in them, from his head to his feet being a nearly straight line. It is difficult to compare the horsemanship of a western plainsman with that of an eastern or southern cross-country rider. In following hounds over fences and high walls, on a spirited horse needing very careful humoring, the latter would certainly excel; but he would find it hard work to sit a bucking horse like a cowboy, or to imitate the headlong dash with which one will cut out a cow marked with his own brand from a herd of several hundred others, or will follow at full speed the twistings and doublings of a refractory steer over ground where an eastern horse would hardly keep its feet walking.

My own ranches, the Elkhorn and the Chimney Butte, lie along the eastern border of the cattle country, where the Little Missouri flows through the heart of the Bad Lands. This, like most other plains rivers, has a broad, shallow bed, through which in times of freshets runs a muddy torrent, that neither man nor beast can pass; at other seasons of the year it is very shallow, spreading out into pools, between which the trickling water may be but a few inches deep. Even then, however, it is not always easy to cross, for the bottom is filled with quicksands and mud-holes. The river flows in long sigmoid curves through an alluvial valley of no great width. The amount of this alluvial land enclosed by a single bend is called a bottom, which may be either covered with cotton-wood trees or else be simply a great grass meadow. From the edges of the valley the land rises abruptly in steep high buttes whose crests are sharp and jagged. This broken country extends back from the river for many miles, and has been called always, by Indians, French voyageurs, and American trappers alike, the "Bad Lands," partly from its dreary and forbidding aspect and partly from the difficulty experienced in travelling through it. Every few miles it is crossed by creeks which open into the Little Missouri, of which they are simply repetitions in miniature, except that during most of the year they are almost dry, some of them having in their beds here and there a never-failing spring or muddy alkaline-water hole. From these creeks run coulies, or narrow, winding valleys, through which water flows when the snow melts; their bottoms contain patches of brush, and they lead back into the heart of the Bad Lands. Some of the buttes spread out into level plateaus, many miles in extent; others form chains, or rise as steep isolated masses. Some are of volcanic origin, being composed of masses of scoria; the others, of sandstone or clay, are worn by water into the most fantastic shapes. In coloring they are as bizarre as in form. Among the level, parallel strata which make up the land are some of coal. When a coal vein gets on fire it makes what is called a burning mine, and the clay above it is turned into brick; so that where water wears away the side of a hill sharp streaks of black and red are seen across it, mingled with the grays, purples, and browns. Some of the buttes are overgrown with gnarled, stunted cedars or small pines, and they are all cleft through and riven in every direction by deep narrow ravines, or by canyons with perpendicular sides.

In spite of their look of savage desolation, the Bad Lands make a good cattle country, for there is plenty of nourishing grass and excellent shelter from the winter storms. The cattle keep close to them in the cold months, while in the summer time they wander out on the broad prairies stretching back of them, or come down to the river bottoms.

My home ranch-house stands on the river brink. From the low, long veranda, shaded by leafy cottonwoods, one looks across sand bars and shallows to a strip of meadowland, behind which rises a line of sheer cliffs and grassy plateaus. This veranda is a pleasant place in the summer evenings when a cool breeze stirs along the river and blows in the faces of the tired men, who loll back in their rocking-chairs (what true American does not enjoy a rocking-chair?), book in hand—though they do not often read the books, but rock gently to and fro, gazing sleepily out at the weird-looking buttes opposite, until their sharp outlines grow indistinct and purple in the after-glow of the sunset. The story-high house of hewn logs is clean and neat, with many rooms, so that one can be alone if one wishes to. The nights in summer are cool and

33

pleasant, and there are plenty of bear-skins and buffalo robes, trophies of our own skill, with which to bid defiance to the bitter cold of winter. In summer time we are not much within doors, for we rise before dawn and work hard enough to be willing to go to bed soon after nightfall. The long winter evenings are spent sitting round the hearthstone, while the pine logs roar and crackle, and the men play checkers or chess, in the fire light. The rifles stand in the corners of the room or rest across the elk antlers which jut out from over the fireplace. From the deer horns ranged along the walls and thrust into the beams and rafters hang heavy overcoats of wolf-skin or coon-skin, and otter-fur or beaver-fur caps and gauntlets. Rough board shelves hold a number of books, without which some of the evenings would be long indeed. No ranchman who loves sport can afford to be without Van Dyke's *Still Hunter,* Dodge's *Plains of the Great West,* or Caton's *Deer and Antelope of America,* and Coues' *Birds of the Northwest* will be valued if he cares at all for natural history. A western plainsman is reminded every day, by the names of the prominent landmarks among which he rides, that the country was known to men who spoke French long before any of his own kinsfolk came to it, and hence he reads with a double interest Parkman's histories of the early Canadians. As for Irving, Hawthorne, Cooper, Lowell, and the other standbys, I suppose no man, east or west, would willingly be long without them; while for lighter reading there are dreamy Ike Marvel, Burroughs' breezy pages, and the quaint, pathetic character-sketches of the Southern Writers—

Cable, Cradock, Macon, Joel Chandler Harris, and sweet Sherwood Bonner. And when one is in the Bad Lands he feels as if they somehow *look* just exactly as Poe's tales and poems *sound*.

By the way, my books have some rather unexpected foes, in the shape of the pack rats. These are larger than our house rats, with soft gray fur, big eyes, and bushy tails, like a squirrel's; they are rather pretty beasts and very tame, often coming into the shacks and log-cabins of the settlers. Woodmen and plainsmen, in their limited vocabulary, make great use of the verb "pack," which means to carry, more properly to carry on one's back; and these rats were christened pack rats, on account of their curious and inveterate habit of dragging off to their holes every object they can possibly move. From the hole of one, underneath the wall of a hut, I saw taken a small revolver, a hunting-knife, two books, a fork, a small bag, and a tin cup. The little shack mice are much more common than the rats, and among them there is a wee pocket-mouse, with pouches on the outside of its little cheeks.

In the spring, when the thickets are green, the hermit thrushes sing sweetly in them; when it is moonlight, the voluble, cheery notes of the thrashers or brown thrushes can be heard all night long. One of our sweetest, loudest songsters is the meadow-lark; this I could hardly get used to at first, for it looks exactly like the eastern meadow-lark, which utters nothing but a harsh, disagreeable chatter. But the plains air seems to give it a voice, and it will perch on the top of a bush

35

or tree and sing for hours in rich, bubbling tones.
Out on the prairie there are several kinds of plains
sparrows which sing very brightly, one of them
hovering in the air all the time, like a bobolink.
Sometimes in the early morning, when crossing the
open, grassy plateaus, I have heard the prince of
them all, the Missouri skylark. The skylark sings
on the wing, soaring over head and mounting in
spiral curves until it can hardly be seen, while its
bright, tender strains never cease for a moment.
I have sat on my horse and listened to one singing
for a quarter of an hour at a time without stopping.
There is another bird also which sings on the wing,
though I have not seen the habit put down in the
books. One bleak March day, when snow covered
the ground and the shaggy ponies crowded about
the empty corral, a flock of snow-buntings came
familiarly round the cow-shed, clambering over
the ridge-pole and roof. Every few moments one of
them would mount into the air, hovering about
with quivering wings and warbling a loud, merry
song with some very sweet notes. They were a most
welcome little group of guests, and we were sorry
when after loitering around a day or two, they
disappeared toward their breeding haunts.

In the still fall nights, if we lie awake we can listen
to the clanging cries of the water-fowl, as their
flocks speed southward; and in cold weather the
coyotes occasionally come near enough for us to
hear their uncanny wailing. The larger wolves, too,
now and then join in, with a kind of deep, dismal
howling; but this melancholy sound is more often
heard when out camping than from the ranchhouse.

The charm of ranch life comes in its freedom, and the vigorous, open-air existence it forces a man to lead. Except when hunting in bad ground, the whole time away from the house is spent in the saddle, and there are so many ponies that a fresh one can always be had. These ponies are of every size and disposition, and rejoice in names as different as their looks. Hackamore, Wire Fence, Steel-Trap, War Cloud, Pinto, Buckskin, Circus, and Standing Jimmie are among those that, as I write, are running frantically round the corral in the vain effort to avoid the rope, wielded by the dextrous and sinewy hand of a broad-hatted cowboy.

A ranchman is kept busy most of the time, but his hardest work comes during the spring and fall round-ups, when the calves are branded or the beeves gathered for market. Our round-up district includes the Beaver and Little Beaver creeks (both of which always contain running water, and head up toward each other), and as much of the river, nearly two hundred miles in extent, as lies between their mouths. All the ranches along the line of these two creeks and the river space between join in sending from one to three or four men to the round-up, each man taking eight ponies; and for every six or seven men there will be a four-horse wagon to carry the blankets and mess kit. The whole, including perhaps forty or fifty cowboys, is under the head of one first-class foreman, styled the captain of the round-up. Beginning at one end of the line the round-up works along clear to the other. Starting at the head of one creek, the wagons and the herd of spare ponies go down it ten or twelve miles, while the cowboys, divided into small parties, scour the neighboring country, covering a great extent of territory, and in the evening come into the appointed place with all the cattle they have seen. This big herd, together with the pony herd, is guarded and watched all night, and driven during the day. At each home-ranch (where there is always a large corral fitted for the purpose) all the cattle of that brand are cut out from the rest of the herd, which is to continue its journey, and the cows and calves are driven into the corral, where the latter are roped, thrown, and branded. In throwing the rope from horseback, the loop, held in the right hand, is swung round and round the head by a motion of the wrist; when on foot, the hand is usually held by the side, the loop dragging on the ground. It is a pretty sight to see a man who knows how, use the rope; again and again an expert will catch fifty animals by the leg without making a misthrow. But unless practice is begun very young it is hard to become really proficient.

Cutting out cattle, next to managing a stampeded herd at night, is that part of the cowboy's work needing the boldest and most skillful horseman-ship. A young heifer or steer is very loath to leave the herd, always tries to break back into it, can run like a deer, and can dodge like a rabbit; but a thorough cattle pony enjoys the work as much as its rider, and follows a beast like a four-footed fate through every double and turn. The ponies for the cutting-out or afternoon work are small and quick; those used for the circle-riding in the morning have need rather to be strong and rangey.

The work on a round-up is very hard, but although the busiest it is also the pleasantest part of a cowboy's existence. His food is good, though coarse, and his sleep is sound indeed; while the work is very exciting, and is done in company, under the stress of an intense rivalry between all the men, both as to their own skill, and as to the speed and training of their horses. Clumsiness, and still more the slightest approach to timidity, expose a man to the roughest and most merciless raillery; and the unfit are weeded out by a very rapid process of natural selection. When the work is over for the day the men gather round the fire for an hour or two to sing songs, talk, smoke, and tell stories; and he who has a good voice, or, better still, can play a fiddle or banjo, is sure to receive his meed of most sincere homage.

Though the ranchman is busiest during the round-up, yet he is far from idle at other times. He rides round among the cattle to see if any are sick, visits any outlying camp of his men, hunts up any band of ponies which may stray—and they are always straying,—superintends the haying, and, in fact, does not often find that he has too much leisure time on his hands. Even in winter he has work which must be done. His ranch supplies milk, butter, eggs, and potatoes, and his rifle keeps him, at least intermittently, in fresh meat; but coffee, sugar, flour, and whatever else he may want, has to be hauled in, and this is generally done when the ice will bear. Then firewood must be chopped; or, if there is a good coal vein, as on my ranch, the coal must be dug out and hauled in. Altogether, though the ranchman will have time enough to take shooting trips, he will be very far from having time to make shooting a business, as a stranger who comes for nothing else can afford to do.

There are now no Indians left in my immediate neighborhood, though a small party of harmless Grosventres occasionally passes through; yet it is but six years since the Sioux surprised and killed five men in a log station just south of me, where the Fort Keogh trail crosses the river; and, two years ago, when I went down on the prairies toward the Black Hills, there was still danger from Indians. That summer the buffalo hunters had killed a couple of Crows, and while we were on the prairie a long-range skirmish occurred near us between some Cheyennes and a number of cowboys. In fact, we ourselves were one day scared by what we thought to be a party of Sioux; but on riding toward them they proved to be half-breed Crees, who were more afraid of us than we were of them.

During the past century a good deal of sentimental nonsense has been talked about our taking the Indians' land. Now, I do not mean to say for a moment that gross wrong has not been done the Indians, both by government and individuals, again and again. The government makes promises impossible to perform, and then fails to do even what it might toward their fulfilment; and where brutal and reckless frontiersmen are brought into contact with a set of treacherous, revengeful, and fiendishly cruel savages a long series of outrages by both sides is sure to follow. But as regards taking the land, at least from the western Indians, the simple truth is that the latter never had any real ownership in it at all. Where the game was plenty, there they hunted; they followed it when it moved away to new hunting-grounds, unless they were prevented by stronger rivals; and to most of the land on which we found them they had no stronger claim than that of having a few years previously butchered the original occupants. When my cattle came to the Little Missouri the region was only inhabited by a score or so of white hunters; their title to it was quite as good as that of most Indian tribes to the lands they claim; yet nobody dreamed of saying that these hunters owned the country. Each could eventually have kept his own claim of 160 acres, and no more. The Indians should be treated in just the same way that we treat the white settlers. Give each his little claim; if, as would generally happen, he declined this, why then let him share the fate of the thousands of white hunters and trappers who have lived on the game that the settlement of the country has exterminated, and let him, like these whites, who will not work, perish from the face of the earth which he cumbers.

The doctrine seems merciless, and so it is; but it is just and rational for all that. It does not do to be merciful to a few, at the cost of justice to the many. The cattle-men at least keep herds and build houses on the land; yet I would not for a moment debar settlers from the right of entry to the cattle country, though their coming in means in the end the destruction of us and our industry.

For we ourselves, and the life that we lead, will shortly pass away from the plains as completely as the red and white hunters who have vanished from before our herds. The free, open-air life of the ranchman, the pleasantest and healthiest life in America, is from its very nature ephemeral. The broad and boundless prairies have already been bounded and will soon be made narrow. It is scarcely a figure of speech to say that the tide of white settlement during the last few years has risen over the west like a flood; and the cattle-men are but the spray from the crest of the wave, thrown far in advance, but soon to be overtaken. As the settlers throng into the lands and seize the good ground, especially that near the streams, the great fenceless ranches, where the cattle and their mounted herdsmen wandered unchecked over hundreds of thousands of acres, will be broken up and divided into corn land, or else into small grazing farms where a few hundred head of stock are closely watched and taken care of. Of course the most powerful ranches, owned by wealthy corporations or individuals, and already firmly rooted in the soil, will long resist this crowding; in places, where the ground is not suited to agriculture, or where, through the old Spanish land-grants, title has been acquired to a great tract of territory, cattle ranching will continue for a long time, though in a greatly modified form; elsewhere I doubt if it outlasts the present century. Immense sums of money have been made at it in the past, and it is still fairly profitable; but the good grounds (aside from those reserved for the Indians) are now almost all taken up, and it is too late for new men to start at it on their own account, unless in exceptional cases, or where an Indian reservation is thrown open. Those that are now in will continue to make money; but most of those who hereafter take it up will lose.

The profits of the business are great; but the chances for loss are great also. A winter of unusual severity will work sad havoc among the young cattle, especially the heifers; sometimes a disease like the Texas cattle fever will take off a whole herd; and many animals stray and are not recovered. In fall, when the grass is like a mass of dry and brittle tinder, the fires do much damage, reducing the prairies to blackened deserts as far as the eye can see, and destroying feed which would keep many thousand head of stock during winter. Then we hold in about equal abhorrence the granger who may come in to till the land, and the sheep-owner who drives his flocks over it. The former will gradually fill up the country to our own exclusion, while the latter's sheep nibble the grass off so close to the ground as to starve out all other animals.

Then we suffer some loss—in certain regions very severe loss—from wild beasts, such as cougars, wolves, and lynxes. The latter, generally called "bob-cats," merely make inroads on the hen-roosts (one of them destroyed half my poultry, coming night after night with most praiseworthy regularity), but the cougars and wolves destroy many cattle.

The wolf is not very common with us; nothing like as plentiful as the little coyote. A few years ago both

43

wolves and coyotes were very numerous on the plains, and as Indians and hunters rarely molested them, they were then very unsuspicious. But all this is changed now. When the cattle-men came in they soon perceived in the wolves their natural foes, and followed them unrelentingly. They shot at and chased them on all occasions, and killed great numbers by poisoning; and as a consequence the comparatively few that are left are as wary and cunning beasts as exist anywhere. They hardly ever stir abroad by day, and hence are rarely shot or indeed seen. During the last three years these brutes have killed nearly a score of my cattle, and in return we have poisoned six or eight wolves and a couple of dozen coyotes; yet in all our riding we have not seen so much as a single wolf, and only rarely a coyote. The coyotes kill sheep and occasionally very young calves, but never meddle with any thing larger. The stockman fears only the large wolves.

According to my experience, the wolf is rather solitary. A single one or a pair will be found by themselves, or possibly with one or more well-grown young ones, and will then hunt over a large tract where no other wolves will be found; and as they wander very far, and as their melancholy howlings have a most ventriloquial effect, they are often thought to be much more plentiful than they are. During the daytime they lie hid in caves or in some patch of bush, and will let a man pass right by them without betraying their presence. Occasionally somebody runs across them by accident. A neighboring ranchman to me once stumbled, while riding an unshod pony, right into the midst of four wolves who were lying in some tall, rank grass, and shot one with his revolver and crippled another before they could get away.

But such an accident as this is very rare; and when, by any chance, the wolf is himself abroad in the daytime he keeps such a sharp look-out, and is so wary, that it is almost impossible to get near him, and he gives every human being a wide berth. At night it is different. The wolves then wander far and wide, often coming up round the out-buildings of the ranches; I have seen in light snow the tracks of two that had walked round the house within fifty feet of it. I have never heard of an instance where a man was attacked or threatened by them, but they will at times kill every kind of domestic animal. They are fond of trying to catch young foals, but do not often succeed, for the mares and foals keep together in a kind of straggling band, and the foal is early able to run at good speed for a short distance. When attacked, the mare and foal dash off towards the rest of the band, which gathers together at once, the foals pressing into the middle and the mares remaining on the outside, not in a ring with their heels out, but moving in and out, and forming a solid mass into which the wolves do not venture. Full-grown horses are rarely molested, while a stallion becomes himself the assailant.

In early spring when the cows begin to calve the wolves sometimes wait upon the herds as they did of old on the buffalo, and snap up any calf that strays away from its mother. When hard pressed by hunger they will kill a steer or a heifer, choosing the bitterest and coldest night to make the attack. The prey is invariably seized by the haunch or flank, and its entrails afterwards torn out; while a cougar, on the contrary, grasps the neck or throat. Wolves have very strong teeth and jaws and inflict a most severe bite. They will in winter come up to the yards and carry away a sheep, pig, or dog without much difficulty; I have known one which had tried to seize a sheep and been prevented by the sheep dogs to canter off with one of the latter instead. But a spirited dog will always attack a wolf. On the ranch next below mine there was a plucky bull terrier, weighing about twenty-five pounds, who lost his life owing to his bravery. On one moonlight night three wolves came round the stable, and the terrier sallied out promptly. He made such a quick rush as to take his opponents by surprise, and seized one by the throat; nor did he let go till the other two tore him almost asunder across the loins. Better luck attended a large mongrel called a sheep dog by his master, but whose blood was apparently about equally derived from collie, Newfoundland, and bulldog. He was a sullen, but very intelligent and determined brute, powerfully built and with strong jaws, and though neither as tall nor as heavy as a wolf he had yet killed two of these animals single-handed. One of them had come into the farm-yard at night, and had taken a young pig, whose squeals roused everybody. The wolf loped off with his booty, the dog running after and overtaking him in the darkness. The struggle was short, for the dog had seized the wolf by the throat and the latter could not shake him off, though he made the most desperate efforts, rising on his hind legs and pressing the dog down with his fore paws. This time the victor escaped scatheless, but in his second fight, when he strangled a still larger wolf he was severely punished. The wolf had seized a sheep, when the dog, rushing on him, caused him to leave his quarry. Instead of running he turned to bay at once, taking off one of the assailant's ears with a rapid snap. The dog did not get a good hold, and the wolf scored him across the shoulders and flung him off. They then faced each other for a minute and at the next dash the dog made good his throat hold, and throttled the wolf, though the latter contrived to get his foe's foreleg into his jaws and broke it clear through. When I saw the dog he had completely recovered, although pretty well scarred.

On another neighboring ranch there is a most ill-favored hybrid, whose mother was a Newfoundland and whose father was a large wolf. It is stoutly built, with erect ears, pointed muzzle, rather short head, short bushy tail, and of a brindled color; funnily enough it looks more like a hyena than like either of its parents. It is familiar with people and a good cattle dog, but rather treacherous; it both barks and howls. The parent wolf carried on a long courtship with the Newfoundland. He came round the ranch, regularly and boldly, every night, and she would at once go out to him. In the daylight he would lie hid in the bushes at some little distance. Once or twice his hiding-place was discovered and then the men would amuse themselves by setting the Newfoundland on him. She would make at him with great apparent ferocity; but when they were a good way from the men he would turn round and wait for her and they would go romping off together, not to be seen again for several hours.

The cougar is hardly ever seen round my ranch; but toward the mountains it is very destructive both to horses and horned cattle. The ranchmen know it by the name of mountain lion; and it is the same beast that in the east is called panther or "painter." The cougar is the same size and build as the Old World leopard, and with very much the same habits. One will generally lie in wait for the heifers or young steers as they come down to water, and singling out an animal, reach it in a couple of bounds and fasten its fangs in the throat or neck. I have seen quite a large cow that had been killed by a cougar; and on another occasion, while out hunting over light snow, I came across a place where two bucks, while fighting, had been stalked up to by a cougar which pulled down one and tore him in pieces. The cougar's gait is silent and stealthy to an extraordinary degree; the look of the animal when creeping up to his prey has been wonderfully caught by the sculptor, Kemeys, in his bronzes: *The Still Hunt* and *The Silent Footfall.*

I have never myself killed a cougar, though my brother shot one in Texas, while still-hunting some deer, which the cougar itself was after. It never attacks man, and even when hard pressed and wounded turns to bay with extreme reluctance, and at the first chance again seeks safety in flight.

48

This was certainly not the case in old times, but the nature of the animal has been so changed by constant contact with rifle-bearing hunters, that timidity toward them has become a hereditary trait deeply engrained in its nature. When the continent was first settled, and for long afterward, the cougar was quite as dangerous an antagonist as the African or Indian leopard, and would even attack men unprovoked. An instance of this occurred in the annals of my mother's family. Early in the present century one of my ancestral relatives, a Georgian, moved down to the wild and almost unknown country bordering on Florida. His plantation was surrounded by jungles in which all kinds of wild beasts swarmed. One of his negroes had a sweetheart on another plantation, and in visiting her, instead of going by the road he took a short cut through the swamps, heedless of the wild beasts, and armed only with a long knife—for he was a man of colossal strength, and of fierce and determined temper. One night he started to return late, expecting to reach the plantation in time for his daily task on the morrow. But he never reached home, and it was thought he had run away. However, when search was made for him his body was found in the path through the swamp, all gashed and torn, and but a few steps from him the body of a cougar, stabbed and cut in many places. Certainly that must have been a grim fight, in the gloomy, lonely recesses of the swamp, with no one to watch the midnight death struggle between the powerful, naked man and the ferocious brute that was his almost unseen assailant.

When hungry, a cougar will attack any thing it can master. I have known of their killing wolves and large dogs. A friend of mine, a ranchman in Wyoming, had two grizzly bear cubs in his possession at one time, and they were kept in a pen outside the ranch. One night two cougars came down, and after vain efforts to catch a dog which was on the place, leaped into the pen and carried off the two young bears!

Two or three powerful dogs, however, will give a cougar all he wants to do to defend himself. A relative of mine in one of the Southern States had a small pack of five blood-hounds, with which he used to hunt the canebrakes for bear, wildcats, etc. On one occasion they ran across a cougar, and after a sharp chase treed him. As the hunters drew near he leaped from the the tree and made off, but was overtaken by the hounds and torn to pieces after a sharp struggle in which one or two of the pack were badly scratched.

Cougars are occasionally killed by poisoning, and they may be trapped much more easily than a wolf. I have never known them to be systematically hunted in the West, though now and then one is accidentally run across and killed with the rifle while the hunter is after some other game.

As already said, ranchmen do not have much idle time on their hands, for their duties are manifold, and they need to be ever on the watch against their foes, both animate and inanimate. Where a man has so much to do he cannot spare a great deal of his time for any amusement; but a good part of that which the ranchman can spare he is very apt to spend in hunting. His quarry will be one of the seven kinds of plains game—bear, buffalo, elk, bighorn, antelope, blacktail or whitetail deer. Moose, caribou, and white goat never come down into the cattle country; and it is only on the southern ranches near the Rio Grande and the Rio Colorado that the truculent peccary and the great spotted jaguar are found.

Until recently all sporting on the plains was confined to army officers, or to men of leisure who made extensive trips for no other purpose; leaving out of consideration the professional hunters, who trapped and shot for their livelihood. But with the incoming of the cattle-men, there grew up a class of residents, men with a stake in the welfare of the country, and with a regular business carried on in it, many of whom were keenly devoted to sport,— a class whose members were in many respects closely akin to the old Southern planters. In this book I propose to give some description of the kind of sport that can be had by the average ranchman who is fond of the rifle. Of course no man with a regular business can have such opportunities as fall to the lot of some who pass their lives in hunting only; and we cannot pretend to equal the achievements of such men, for with us it is merely a pleasure, to be eagerly sought after when we have the chance, but not to be allowed to interfere with our business. No ranchmen have time to make such extended trips as are made by some devotees of sport who are so fortunate as to have no every-day work to which to attend. Still, ranch life undoubtedly offers more chance to a man to get sport than is now the case with any other occupation in America, and those who follow it are apt to be men of game spirit, fond of excitement and adventure, who perforce lead an open-air life, who must needs ride well, for they are often in the saddle from sunrise to sunset, and who naturally take kindly to that noblest of weapons, the rifle. With such men hunting is one of the chief of pleasures; and they follow it eagerly when their work will allow them. And with some of them it is at times more than a pleasure. On many of the ranches—on my own, for instance—the supply of fresh meat depends mainly on the skill of the riflemen, and so, both for pleasure and profit, most ranchmen do a certain amount of hunting each season. The buffalo are now gone forever, and the elk are rapidly sharing their fate; but antelope and deer are still quite plenty, and will remain so for some years; and these are the common game of the plainsman. Nor is it likely that the game will disappear much before ranch life itself is a thing of the past. It is a phase of American life as fascinating as it is evanescent, and one well deserving an historian. But in these pages I propose to dwell on only one of its many pleasant sides, and give some idea of the game shooting which forms perhaps the chief of the cattle-man's pleasures, aside from those more strictly connected with his actual work. I have to tell of no unusual adventures, but merely of just such hunting as lies within reach of most of the sport-loving ranchmen whose cattle range along the waters of the Powder and the Bighorn, the Little Missouri and the Yellowstone.

Of course I have never myself gone out hunting under the direction of a professional guide or professional hunter, unless it was to see one of the latter who was reputed a crack shot; all of my trips have been made either by myself or else with one of my cowboys as a companion. Most of the so-called hunters are not worth much. There are plenty of men hanging round the frontier settlements who claim to be hunters, and who bedizen themselves in all the traditional finery of the craft, in the hope of getting a job at guiding some "tender-foot"; and there are plenty of skin-hunters, or meat-hunters, who, after the Indians have been driven away and when means of communication have been established, mercilessly slaughter the game in season and out, being too lazy to work at any regular trade, and keeping on hunting until the animals become too scarce and shy to be taken without more skill than they possess; but these are all mere temporary excrescences, and the true old Rocky Mountain hunter and trapper, the plainsman, or mountain-man, who, with all his faults, was a man of iron nerve and will, is now almost a thing of the past. In the place of these heroes of a bygone age, the men who were clad in buckskin and who carried long rifles, stands, or rather rides, the bronzed and sinewy cowboy, as picturesque and self-reliant, as dashing and resolute as the saturnine Indian fighters whose place he has taken; and, alas that it should be written! he in his turn must at no distant time share the fate of the men he has displaced. The ground over which he so gallantly rides his small, wiry horse will soon know him no more, and in his stead there will be the plodding grangers and husbandmen. I suppose it is right and for the best that the great cattle country, with its broad extent of fenceless land, over which the ranchman rides as free as the game that he follows or the horned herds that he guards, should be in the end broken up into small patches of fenced farm land and grazing land; but I hope against hope that I myself shall not live to see this take place, for when it does one of the pleasantest and freest phases of western American life will have come to an end.

The old hunters were a class by themselves. They penetrated, alone or in small parties, to the farthest and wildest haunts of the animals they followed, leading a solitary, lonely life, often never seeing a white face for months and even years together. They were skilful shots, and were cool, daring, and resolute to the verge of recklessness. On any thing like even terms they very greatly overmatched the Indians by whom they were surrounded, and with whom they waged constant and ferocious war. In the government expeditions against the plains tribes they were of absolutely invaluable assistance as scouts. They rarely had regular wives or white children, and there are none to take their places, now that the greater part of them have gone. For the men who carry on hunting as a business where it is perfectly safe have all the vices of their prototypes, but, not having to face the dangers that beset the latter, so neither need nor possess the stern, rough virtues that were required in order to meet and overcome them. The ranks of the skin-hunters and meat-hunters contain some good men; but as a rule they are a most unlovely race of beings, not excelling even in the pursuit which they follow because they are too shiftless to do any thing else; and the sooner they vanish the better.

A word as to weapons and hunting dress. When I first came to the plains I had a heavy Sharps rifle, 45-120, shooting an ounce and a quarter of lead, and a 50-calibre, double-barrelled English express. Both of these, especially the latter, had a vicious recoil; the former was very clumsy; and above all they were neither of them repeaters; for a repeater or magazine gun is as much superior to a single- or double-barrelled breech-loader as the latter is to a muzzle-loader. I threw them both aside: and have instead a 40-90 Sharps for very long range work; a 50-115 6-shot Bullard express, which has the velocity, shock, and low trajectory of the English gun; and, better than either, a 45-75 half-magazine Winchester. The Winchester, which is stocked and sighted to suit myself, is by all odds the best weapon I ever had, and I now use it almost exclusively, having killed every kind of game with it, from a grizzly bear to a big-horn. It is as handy to carry, whether on foot or on horseback, and comes up to the shoulder as readily as a shot-gun; it is absolutely sure, and there is no recoil to jar and disturb the aim, while it carries accurately quite as far as a man can aim with any degree of certainty; and the bullet, weighing three quarters of an ounce, is plenty large enough for any thing on this continent. For shooting the very large game (buffalo, elephants, etc.) of India and South Africa, much heavier rifles are undoubtedly necessary; but the Winchester is the best gun for any game to be found in the United States, for it is as deadly, accurate, and handy as any, stands very rough usage, and is unapproachable for the rapidity of its fire and the facility with which it is loaded.

Of course every ranchman carries a revolver, a long 45 Colt or Smith & Wesson, by preference the former. When after game a hunting-knife is stuck in the girdle. This should be stout and sharp, but not too long, with a round handle. I have two double-barrelled shot-guns: a No. 10 choke-bore for ducks and geese, made by Thomas of Chicago; and a No. 16 hammerless, built for me by Kennedy of St. Paul, for grouse and plover. On regular hunting trips I always carry the Winchester rifle; but in riding round near home, where a man may see a deer and is sure to come across ducks and grouse, it is best to take the little ranch gun, a double-barrel No. 16, with a 40-70 rifle underneath the shot-gun barrels.

As for clothing, when only off on a day's trip, the ordinary ranchman's dress is good enough: flannel shirt, and overalls tucked into alligator boots, the latter being of service against the brambles, cacti, and rattlesnakes. Such a costume is good in warm weather. When making a long hunting trip, where there will be much rough work, especially in the dry cold of fall and winter, there is nothing better than a fringed buckskin tunic or hunting-shirt, (held in at the waist by the cartridge belt,) buckskin trousers, and a fur cap, with heavy moccasins for use in the woods, and light alligator-hide shoes if it is intended to cross rocks and open ground. Buckskin is most durable, keeps out wind and cold, and is the best possible color for the hunter—no small point in approaching game. For wet it is not as good as flannel, and it is hot in warm weather. On very cold days, fur gloves and either a coon-skin overcoat or a short riding jacket of fisher's fur may be worn. In cold weather, if travelling light with only what can be packed behind the horse, I sleep in a big buffalo-robe, sewed up at the sides and one end into the form of a bag, and very warm. When, as is sometimes the case, the spirit in the thermometer sinks to -60°-65° Fahrenheit, it is necessary to have more wraps and bedding, and we use beaver-robes and bearskins. An oilskin "slicker" or waterproof overcoat and a pair of shaps keep out the rain almost completely.

Where most of the hunting is done on horseback the hunting-pony is a very important animal. Many people seem to think that any broken-down pony will do to hunt, but this seems to me a very great mistake. My own hunting-horse, Manitou, is the best and most valuable animal on the ranch. He is stoutly built and strong, able to carry a good-sized buck behind his rider for miles at a lope without minding it in the least; he is very enduring and very hardy, not only picking up a living but even growing fat when left to shift for himself under very hard conditions; and he is perfectly surefooted and as fast as any horse on the river. Though both willing and spirited, he is very gentle, with an easy mouth, and will stay grazing in one spot when left, and will permit himself to be caught without difficulty. Add to these virtues the fact that he will let any dead beast or thing be packed on him, and will allow a man to shoot off his back or right by him without moving, and it is evident that he is as nearly perfect as can be the case with hunting-horseflesh. There is a little sorrel mare on the ranch, a perfect little pet, that is almost as good, but too small. We have some other horses we frequently use, but all have faults. Some of the quiet ones are slow, lazy, or tire easily; others are gun shy; while others plunge and buck if we try to pack any game on their backs. Others cannot be left standing untied, as they run away; and I can imagine few forms of exercise so soul-harrowing as that of spending an hour or two in running, in shaps, top boots, and spurs over a broken prairie, with the thermometer at 90°, after an escaped horse. Most of the hunting-horses used by my friends have one or more of these tricks, and it is rare to find one, like Manitou, who has none of them. Manitou is a treasure and I value him accordingly. Besides, he is a sociable old fellow, and a great companion when off alone, coming up to have his head rubbed or to get a crust of bread, of which he is very fond.

To be remarkably successful in killing game a man must be a good shot; but a good target shot may be a very poor hunter, and a fairly successful hunter

58

may be only a moderate shot. Shooting well with the rifle is the highest kind of skill, for the rifle is the queen of weapons; and it is a difficult art to learn. But many other qualities go to make up the first-class hunter. He must be persevering, watchful, hardy, and with good judgment; and a little dash and energy at the proper time often help him immensely. I myself am not, and never will be, more than an ordinary shot; for my eyes are bad and my hand not over-steady; yet I have killed every kind of game to be found on the plains, partly because I have hunted very perseveringly, and partly because by practice I have learned to shoot about as well at a wild animal as at a target. I have killed rather more game than most of the ranchmen who are my neighbors, though at least half of them are better shots than I am.

Time and again I have seen a man who had, as he deemed, practised sufficiently at a target, come out "to kill a deer," hot with enthusiasm; and nine out of ten times he has gone back unsuccessful, even when deer were quite plenty. Usually he has been told by the friend who advised him to take the trip, or by the guide who inveigled him into it, that "the deer were so plenty you saw them all round you," and, this not proving quite true, he lacks perseverance to keep on; or else he fails to see the deer at the right time; or else if he does see it he misses it, making the discovery that to shoot at a gray object, not overdistinctly seen, at a distance merely guessed at, and with a background of other gray objects, is very different from firing into a target, brightly painted and a fixed number of yards off. A man must be able to hit a bull's-eye eight inches across every time to do good work with deer or other game; for the spot around the shoulders that is fatal is not much bigger than this; and a shot a little back of that merely makes a wound which may in the end prove mortal, but which will in all probability allow the animal to escape for the time being. It takes a good shot to hit a bull's-eye off-hand several times in succession at a hundred yards, and if the bull's-eye was painted the same color as the rest of the landscape, and was at an uncertain distance, and, moreover, was alive, and likely to take to its heels at any moment, the difficulty of making a good shot would be greatly enhanced. The man who can kill his buck right along at a hundred yards has a right to claim that he is a good shot. If he can shoot off-hand standing up, that is much the best way, but I myself always drop on one knee, if I have time, unless the animal is very close. It is curious to hear the nonsense that is talked and to see the nonsense that is written about the distances at which game is killed. Rifles now carry with deadly effect the distance of a mile, and most middle-range hunting-rifles would at least kill at half a mile; and in war firing is often begun at these ranges. But in war there is very little accurate aiming, and the fact that there is a variation of thirty or forty feet in the flight of the ball makes no difference; and, finally, a thousand bullets are fired for every man that is killed—and usually many more than a thousand. How would that serve for a record on game? The truth is that three hundred yards is a very long shot, and that even two hundred yards is a long shot. On looking over my game-book I find that the average distance at which I have killed game on the plains is less than a hundred and fifty yards. A few years ago, when the buffalo would stand still in great herds, half a mile from the hunter, the latter, using a long-range Sharps rifle, would often, by firing a number of shots into the herd at that distance, knock over two or three buffalo; but I have hardly ever known single animals to be killed six hundred yards off, even in antelope hunting, the kind in which most long-range shooting is done; and at half that distance a very good shot, with all the surroundings in his favor, is more apt to miss than to hit. Of course old hunters—the most inveterate liars on the face of the earth—are all the time telling of their wonderful shots at even longer distances, and they do occasionally, when shooting very often, make them, but their performances, when actually tested, dwindle amazingly. Others, amateurs, will brag of their rifles. I lately read in a magazine about killing antelopes at eight hundred yards with a Winchester express, a weapon which cannot be depended upon at over two hundred, and is wholly inaccurate at over three hundred yards.

The truth is that, in almost all cases the hunter merely guesses at the distance, and, often perfectly honestly, just about doubles it in his own mind. Once a man told me of an extraordinary shot by which he killed a deer at four hundred yards. A couple of days afterward we happened to pass the place, and I had the curiosity to step off the distance, finding it a trifle over a hundred and ninety. I always make it a rule to pace off the distance after a successful shot, whenever practicable—that is, when the animal has not run too far before dropping,—and I was at first both amused and somewhat chagrined to see how rapidly what I had supposed to be remarkably long shots shrank under actual pacing. It is a good rule always to try to get as near the game as possible, and in most cases it is best to risk startling it in the effort to get closer rather than to risk missing it by a shot at long range. At the same time, I am a great believer in powder-burning, and if I cannot get near, will generally try a shot anyhow, if there is a chance of the rifle's carrying to it. In this way a man will now and then, in the midst of many misses, make a very good long shot, but he should not try to deceive himself into the belief that these occasional long shots are to be taken as samples of his ordinary skill. Yet it is curious to see how a really truthful man will forget his misses, and his hits at close quarters, and, by dint of constant repetition, will finally persuade himself that he is in the habit of killing his game at three or four hundred yards. Of course in different kinds of ground the average range for shooting varies. In the Bad Lands most shots will be obtained much closer than on the prairie, and in the timber they will be nearer still.

Old hunters who are hardy, persevering, and well acquainted with the nature of the animals they pursue, will often kill a great deal of game without being particularly good marksmen; besides, they are careful to get up close, and are not flurried at all, shooting as well at a deer as they do at a target. They are, as a rule, fair shots—that is, they shoot a great deal better than Indians or soldiers, or than the general run of Eastern amateur sportsmen; but I have never been out with one who has not missed a great deal, and the"Leather-stocking"class of shooting stories are generally untrue, at least to the extent of suppressing part of the truth—that is, the number of misses. Beyond question our Western hunters are, as a body, to the full as good marksmen as, and probably much better than, any other body of men in the world, not even excepting the Dutch Boers or Tyrolese Jägers, and a certain number of them who shoot a great deal at game, and are able to squander cartridges very freely, undoubtedly become crack shots, and perform really wonderful feats. As an instance there is old"Vic," a former scout and Indian fighter, and concededly the best hunter on the Little Missouri; probably there are not a dozen men in the West who are better shots or hunters than he is, and I have seen him do most skilful work. He can run the muzzle of his rifle through a board so as to hide the sights, and yet do quite good shooting at some little distance; he will cut the head off a chicken at eighty or ninety yards, shoot a deer running through brush at that distance, kill grouse on the wing early in the season, and knock over antelopes when they are so far off that I should not dream of shooting. He firmly believes, and so do most men that speak of him, that he never misses. Yet I have known him make miss after miss at game, and some that were not such especially difficult shots either. One secret of his success is his constant practice. He is firing all the time, at marks, small birds, etc., etc., and will average from fifty to a hundred cartridges a day; he certainly uses nearly twenty thousand a year, while a man who only shoots for sport, and that occasionally, will, in practising at marks and every thing else, hardly get through with five hundred. Besides, he was cradled in the midst of wild life, and has handled a rifle and used it against both brute and human foes almost since his infancy; his nerves and sinews are like iron, and his eye is naturally both quick and true.

Vic is an exception. With practice an amateur will become nearly as good a shot as the average hunter; and, as I said before, I do not myself believe in taking out a professional hunter as a shooting companion. If I do not go alone I generally go with one of my foremen, Merrifield, who himself came from the East but five years ago. He is a good-looking fellow, daring and self-reliant, a good rider and first-class shot, and a very keen sportsman. Of late years he has been my *fidus Achates* of the hunting field. I can kill more game with him than I can alone; and in hunting on the plains there are many occasions on which it is almost a necessity to have a companion along.

It frequently happens that a solitary hunter finds himself in an awkward predicament, from which he could be extricated easily enough if there were another man with him. His horse may fall into a wash-out, or may get stuck in a mud-hole or quicksand in such a manner that a man working by himself will have great difficulty in getting it out; and two heads often prove better than one in an emergency, especially if a man gets hurt in any way.

The first thing that a western plainsman has to learn is the capacity for self-help, but at the same time he must not forget that occasions may arise when the help of others will be most grateful.

Memories of the American Frontier

On the Cattle Ranges: The Prong-Horn Antelope

In a Stampede

An Episode in the Opening Up of a Cattle Country

II
On the Cattle Ranges:
The Prong-Horn Antelope

Early one June just after the close of the regular
spring round-up, a couple of wagons, with a score
of riders between them, were sent to work some
hitherto untouched country, between the Little
Missouri and the Yellowstone. I was to go as the
representative of our own and of one or two
neighboring brands; but as the round-up had
halted near my ranch I determined to spend a day
there, and then to join the wagons;—the appointed
meeting-place being a cluster of red scoria buttes,
some forty miles distant, where there was a
spring of good water.

Most of my day at the ranch was spent in slumber;
for I had been several weeks on the round-up,
where nobody ever gets quite enough sleep. This is
the only drawback to the work; otherwise it is
pleasant and exciting, with just that slight touch of
danger necessary to give it zest, and without the
wearing fatigue of such labor as lumbering or
mining. But there is never enough sleep, at least on
the spring and mid-summer round-ups. The men

are in the saddle from dawn until dusk, at the time
when the days are longest on these great northern
plains; and in addition there is the regular night
guarding and now and then a furious storm or a
stampede, when for twenty-four hours at a stretch
the riders only dismount to change horses or snatch
a mouthful of food.

I started in the bright sunrise, riding one horse and
driving loose before me eight others, one carrying
my bedding. They travelled strung out in single
file. I kept them trotting and loping, for loose
horses are easiest to handle when driven at some
speed, and moreover the way was long. My rifle
was slung under my thigh; the lariat was looped on
the saddle-horn.

At first our trail led through winding coulies, and
sharp grassy defiles; the air was wonderfully clear,
the flowers were in bloom, the breath of the wind in
my face was odorous and sweet. The patter and beat
of the unshod hoofs, rising in half-rhythmic
measure, frightened the scudding deer; but the
yellow-breasted meadow larks, perched on the
budding tops of the bushes, sang their rich full
songs without heeding us as we went by.

When the sun was well on high and the heat of the
day had begun we came to a dreary and barren
plain, broken by rows of low clay buttes. The
ground in places was whitened by alkali; elsewhere
it was dull gray. Here there grew nothing save
sparse tufts of coarse grass, and cactus, and
sprawling sage brush. In the hot air all things seen

afar danced and wavered. As I rode and gazed at
the shimmering haze the vast desolation of the
landscape bore on me; it seemed as if the unseen and
unknown powers of the wastes were moving by and
marshalling their silent forces. No man save the
wilderness dweller knows the strong melancholy
fascination of these long rides through lonely lands.

At noon, that the horses might graze and drink,
I halted where some box-alders grew by a pool
in the bed of a half-dry creek; and shifted my saddle
to a fresh beast. When we started again we came
out on the rolling prairie, where the green sea of
wind-rippled grass stretched limitless as far as the
eye could reach. Little striped gophers scuttled
away, or stood perfectly straight at the mouths of
their burrows, looking like picket pins. Curlews
clamored mournfully as they circled overhead.
Prairie fowl swept off, clucking and calling, or
strutted about with their sharp tails erect. Antelope
were very plentiful, running like race-horses
across the level, or uttering their queer, barking
grunt as they stood at gaze, the white hairs on their
rumps all on end, their neck bands of broken
brown and white vivid in the sunlight. They were
found singly or in small straggling parties; the
master bucks had not yet begun to drive out the
younger and weaker ones as later in the season,
when each would gather into a herd as many does as
his jealous strength could guard from rivals.
The nursing does whose kids had come early were
often found with the bands; the others kept apart.
The kids were very conspicuous figures on the
prairies, across which they scudded like jack

rabbits, showing nearly as much speed and alertness as their parents; only the very young sought safety by lying flat to escape notice.

The horses cantered and trotted steadily over the mat of buffalo grass, steering for the group of low scoria mounds which was my goal. In mid-afternoon I reached it. The two wagons were drawn up near the spring; under them lay the night-wranglers, asleep; nearby the teamster-cooks were busy about the evening meal. A little way off the two day-wranglers were watching the horse-herd; into which I speedily turned my own animals. The riders had already driven in the bunches of cattle; and were engaged in branding the calves, and turning loose the animals that were not needed, while the remainder were kept, forming the nucleus of the herd which was to accompany the wagon.

As soon as the work was over the men rode to the wagons; sinewy fellows, with tattered broad-brimmed hats and clanking spurs, some wearing leather shaps or leggings, others having their trousers tucked into their high-heeled top-boots, all with their flannel shirts and loose neckerchiefs dusty and sweaty. A few were indulging in rough, good-natured horse play, to an accompaniment of yelling mirth; most were grave and taciturn, greeting me with a silent nod or a "How! friend." A very talkative man, unless the acknowledged wit of the party, according to the somewhat florid frontier notion of wit, is always looked on with disfavor in a cow-camp. After supper, eaten in silent haste, we gathered round the embers of the small fires, and the conversation glanced fitfully over the threadbare subjects common to all such camps; the antics of some particularly vicious bucking bronco, how the different brands of cattle were showing up, the smallness of the calf drop, the respective merits of rawhide lariats and grass ropes, and bits of rather startling and violent news concerning the fates of certain neighbors. Then one by one we began to turn in under our blankets.

Our wagon was to furnish the night guards for the cattle; and each of us had his gentlest horse tied ready to hand. The night guards went on duty two at a time for two-hour watches. By good luck my watch came last. My comrade was a happy-go-lucky young Texan who for some inscrutable reason was known as "Latigo Strap"; he had just come from the south with a big drove of trail cattle.

A few minutes before two one of the guards who had gone on duty at midnight rode into camp and wakened us by shaking our shoulders. Fumbling in the dark I speedily saddled my horse; Latigo had left his saddled, and he started ahead of me. One of the annoyances of night guarding, at least in thick weather, is the occasional difficulty of finding the herd after leaving camp, or in returning to camp after the watch is over; there are few things more exasperating than to be helplessly wandering about in the dark under such circumstances. However, on this occasion there was no such trouble; for it was a brilliant starlight night and the herd had been bedded down by a sugar-loaf butte which made a

good landmark. As we reached the spot we could
make out the loom of the cattle lying close together
on the level plain; and then the dim figure of
a horseman rose vaguely from the darkness
and moved by in silence; it was the other of the
two midnight guards, on his way back to his
broken slumber.

At once we began to ride slowly round the cattle in
opposite directions. We were silent, for the night
was clear, and the herd quiet; in wild weather, when
the cattle are restless, the cowboys never cease
calling and singing as they circle them, for the
sounds seem to quiet the beasts.

For over an hour we steadily paced the endless
round, saying nothing, with our great-coats
buttoned, for the air is chill towards morning on
the northern plains, even in summer. Then faint
streaks of gray appeared in the east. Latigo Strap
began to call merrily to the cattle. A coyote came
sneaking over the butte nearby, and halted to yell
and wail; afterwards he crossed the coulie and from
the hillside opposite again shrieked in dismal
crescendo. The dawn brightened rapidly; the little
skylarks of the plains began to sing, soaring far
overhead, while it was still much too dark to see
them. Their song is not powerful, but it is so clear
and fresh and long-continued that it always appeals
to one very strongly; especially because it is most
often heard in the rose-tinted air of the glorious
mornings, while the listener sits in the saddle,
looking across the endless sweep of the prairies.

As it grew lighter the cattle became restless, rising
and stretching themselves, while we continued to
ride round them.

Then the bronc' began to pitch
   And I began to ride;
He bucked me off a cut bank,
   Hell! I nearly died!

sang Latigo from the other side of the herd. A yell
from the wagons told that the cook was summoning
the sleeping cow-punchers to breakfast; we were
soon able to distinguish their figures as they rolled
out of their bedding, wrapped and corded it into
bundles, and huddled sullenly round the little fires.
The horse wranglers were driving in the saddle
bands. All the cattle got on their feet and started
feeding. In a few minutes the hasty breakfast at
the wagons had evidently been despatched for we
could see the men forming rope corrals into which
the ponies were driven; then each man saddled,
bridled, and mounted his horse, two or three
of the half-broken beasts bucking, rearing,
and plunging frantically in the vain effort to
unseat their riders.

The two men who were first in the saddle relieved
Latigo and myself and we immediately galloped to
camp, shifted our saddles to fresh animals, gulped
down a cup or two of hot coffee, and some pork,
beans, and bread, and rode to the spot where the
others were gathered, lolling loosely in their
saddles, and waiting for the round-up boss to

assign them their tasks. We were the last, and as soon as we arrived the boss divided all into two parties for the morning work, or "circle riding," whereby the cattle were to be gathered for the round-up proper. Then, as the others started, he turned to me and remarked: "We've got enough hands to drive this open country without you; but we're out of meat, and I don't want to kill a beef for such a small outfit; can't you shoot some antelope this morning? We'll pitch camp by the big blasted cottonwood at the foot of the ash coulies, over yonder, below the breaks of Dry Creek."

Of course I gladly assented, and was speedily riding alone across the grassy slopes. There was no lack of the game I was after, for from every rise of ground I could see antelope scattered across the prairie, singly, in couples, or in bands. But their very numbers, joined to the lack of cover on such an open, flattish country, proved a bar to success; while I was stalking one band another was sure to see me and begin running, whereat the first would likewise start; I missed one or two very long shots, and noon found me still without game.

However, I was then lucky enough to see a band of a dozen feeding to windward of a small butte, and by galloping in a long circle I got within a quarter of a mile of them before having to dismount. The stalk itself was almost too easy; for I simply walked to the butte, climbed carefully up a slope where the soil was firm and peered over the top to see the herd, a little one, a hundred yards off. They saw me at once and ran, but I held well ahead of a fine

young prong-buck, and rolled him over like a
rabbit, with both shoulders broken. In a few
minutes I was riding onwards once more with the
buck lashed behind my saddle.

The next one I got, a couple of hours later, offered a
much more puzzling stalk. He was a big fellow in
company with four does or small bucks. All five
were lying in the middle of a slight basin, at the
head of a gentle valley. At first sight it seemed
impossible to get near them, for there was not so
much cover as a sage brush, and the smooth,
shallow basin in which they lay was over a thousand
yards across, while they were looking directly
down the valley. However, it is curious how hard it
is to tell, even from nearby, whether a stalk can or
cannot be made; the difficulty being to estimate the
exact amount of shelter yielded by little inequalities
of ground. In this instance a small shallow
watercourse, entirely dry, ran along the valley, and
after much study I decided to try to crawl up it,
although the big bulging telescopic eyes of the
prong-buck—which have much keener sight than
deer or any other game—would in such case be
pointed directly my way.

Having made up my mind I backed cautiously
down form the coign of vantage whence I had first
seen the game, and ran about a mile to the mouth of
a washout which formed the continuation of the
watercourse in question. Protected by the high clay
banks of this washout I was able to walk upright
until within half a mile of the prong-bucks; then
my progress became very tedious and toilsome, as I

79

had to work my way up the watercourse flat on my stomach, dragging the rifle beside me. At last I reached a spot beyond which not even a snake could crawl unnoticed. In front was a low bank, a couple of feet high, crested with tufts of coarse grass. Raising my head very cautiously I peered through these and saw the prong-horn about a hundred and fifty yards distant. At the same time I found that I had crawled to the edge of a village of prairie dogs, which had already made me aware of their presence by their shrill yelping. They saw me at once; and all those away from their homes scuttled towards them, and dived down the burrows, or sat on the mounds at the entrances, scolding convulsively and jerking their fat little bodies and short tails. This commotion at once attracted the attention of the antelope. They rose forthwith, and immediately caught a glimpse of the black muzzle of the rifle which I was gently pushing through the grass tufts. The fatal curiosity which so often in this species offsets wariness and sharp sight, proved my friend; evidently the antelope could not quite make me out and wished to know what I was. They moved nervously to and fro, striking the earth with their fore hoofs, and now and then uttering a sudden bleat. At last the big buck stood still broadside to me, and I fired. He went off with the others, but lagged behind as they passed over the hill crest, and when I reached it I saw him standing, not very far off, with his head down. Then he walked backwards a few steps, fell over on his side, and died.

As he was a big buck I slung him across the saddle, and started for camp afoot, leading the horse.

However my hunt was not over, for while still a mile from the wagons, going down a coulie of Dry Creek, a yearling prong-buck walked over the divide to my right and stood still until I sent a bullet into its chest; so that I made my appearance in camp with three antelope.

I spoke above of the sweet singing of the western meadow lark and plains skylark; neither of them kin to the true skylark, by the way, one being a cousin of the grakles and hang-birds, and the other a kind of pipit. To me both of these birds are among the most attractive singers to which I have ever listened; but with all bird-music much must be allowed for the surroundings, and much for the mood, and the keenness of sense, of the listener. The lilt of the plains skylark is neither very powerful nor very melodious; but it is sweet, pure, long-sustained, with a ring of courage befitting a song uttered in highest air.

The meadow lark is a singer of a higher order, deserving to rank with the best. Its song has length, variety, power and rich melody; and there is in it sometimes a cadence of wild sadness, inexpressibly touching. Yet I cannot say that either song would appeal to others as it appeals to me; for to me it comes forever laden with a hundred memories and associations; with the sight of dim hills reddening in the dawn, with the breath of cool morning winds blowing across lonely plains, with the scent of flowers on the sunlit prairie, with the motion of fiery horses, with all the strong thrill of eager and buoyant life. I doubt if any man can judge dispassionately the bird songs of his own country; he cannot disassociate them from the sights and sounds of the land that is so dear to him.

This is not a feeling to regret, but it must be taken into account in accepting any estimate of bird music—even in considering the reputation of the European skylark and nightingale. To both of these birds I have often listened in their own homes; always with pleasure and admiration, but always with a growing belief that relatively to some other birds they were ranked too high. They are pre-eminently birds with literary associations; most people take their opinions of them at second-hand, from the poets.

No one can help liking the lark; it is such a brave, honest, cheery bird, and moreover its song is uttered in the air, and is very long-sustained. But it is by no means a musician of the first rank. The nightingale is a performer of a very different and far higher order; yet though it is indeed a notable and admirable singer, it is an exaggeration to call it unequalled. In melody, and above all in that finer, higher melody where the chords vibrate with the touch of eternal sorrow, it cannot rank with such singers as the wood thrush and hermit thrush. The serene, ethereal beauty of the hermit's song, rising and falling through the still evening, under the archways of hoary mountain forests that have endured from time everlasting; the golden, leisurely chiming of the wood thrush, sounding on June afternoons, stanza by stanza, through sun-flecked groves of tall hickories, oaks, and chestnuts; with these there is nothing in the nightingale's song to compare. But in volume and continuity, in tuneful, voluble, rapid outpouring and ardor, above all in skilful and intricate variation of theme, its song far surpasses that of either of the thrushes. In all these respects it is more just to compare it with the mocking-bird's, which, as a rule, likewise falls short precisely on those points where the songs of the two thrushes excel.

The mocking-bird is a singer that has suffered much in reputation from its powers of mimicry. On ordinary occasions, and especially in the daytime, it insists on playing the harlequin. But when free in its own favorite haunts at night in the love season it has a song, or rather songs, which are not only purely original, but are also more beautiful than any other bird music whatsoever. Once I listened to a mocking-bird singing the livelong spring night, under the full moon, in a magnolia tree; and I do not think I shall ever forget its song.

It was on the plantation of Major Campbell Brown, near Nashville, in the beautiful, fertile mid-Tennessee country. The mocking-birds were prime favorites on the place; and were given full scope for the development, not only of their bold friendliness towards mankind, but also of that marked individuality and originality of character in which they so far surpass every other bird as to become the most interesting of all feathered folk. One of the mockers, which lived in the hedge bordering the garden, was constantly engaged in an amusing feud with an honest old setter dog, the point of attack being the tip of the dog's tail. For some reason the bird seemed to regard any hoisting of the setter's tail as a challenge and insult. It would flutter near the dog as he walked; the old setter would become interested in something and raise his tail. The bird would promptly fly at it and peck the tip; whereupon down went the tail until in a couple of minutes the old fellow would forget himself, and the scene would be repeated. The dog usually bore the assaults with comic resignation; and the mocker easily avoided any momentary outburst of clumsy resentment.

On the evening in question the moon was full. My host kindly assigned me a room of which the windows opened on a great magnolia tree, where, I was told, a mocking-bird sang every night and all night long. I went to my room about ten. The moonlight was shining in through the open window, and the mocking-bird was already in the magnolia. The great tree was bathed in a flood of shining silver; I could see each twig, and mark every action of the singer, who was pouring forth such a rapture of ringing melody as I have never listened to before or since. Sometimes he would perch motionless for many minutes, his body quivering and thrilling with the outpour of music. Then he would drop softly from twig to twig, until the lowest limb was reached, when he would rise, fluttering and leaping through the branches, his song never ceasing for an instant, until he reached the summit of the tree and launched into the warm, scent-laden air, floating in spirals, with outspread wings, until, as if spent, he sank gently back into the tree and down through the branches, while his song rose into an ecstasy of ardor and passion. His voice rang like a clarionet, in rich, full tones, and his execution covered the widest possible compass; theme followed theme, a torrent of music, a swelling tide of harmony, in which scarcely any two bars were alike. I stayed till midnight listening to him; he was singing when I went to sleep; he was still singing when I woke a couple of hours later; he sang through the livelong night.

There are many singers beside the meadow lark and little skylark in the plains country; that brown and desolate land, once the home of the thronging buffalo, still haunted by the bands of the prong-buck, and roamed over in ever increasing numbers by the branded herds of the ranchman. In the brush of the river bottoms there are the thrasher and song sparrow; on the grassy uplands the lark finch, vesper sparrow, and lark bunting; and in the rough canyons the rock wren, with its ringing melody.

Yet in certain moods a man cares less for even the loveliest bird songs than for the wilder, harsher, stronger sounds of the wilderness; the guttural booming and clucking of the prairie fowl and the great sage fowl in spring; the honking of gangs of wild geese, as they fly in rapid wedges; the bark of an eagle, wheeling in the shadow of storm-scarred cliffs; or the far-off clanging of many sand-hill cranes, soaring high overhead in circles which cross and recross at an incredible altitude.

Wilder yet, and stranger, are the cries of the great four-footed beasts; the rhythmic pealing of a bull-elk's challenge; and that most sinister and mournful sound, ever fraught with foreboding of murder and rapine, the long-drawn baying of the gray wolf.

Indeed, save to the trained ear most mere bird songs are not very noticeable. The ordinary wilderness dweller, whether hunter or cowboy, scarcely heeds them; and in fact knows but little of the smaller birds. If a bird has some conspicuous peculiarity of look or habit he will notice its existence; but not otherwise. He knows a good deal about magpies, whiskey jacks, or water ousels; but nothing whatever concerning the thrushes, finches, and warblers.

It is the same with mammals. The prairie-dogs he cannot help noticing. With the big pack-rats also he is well acquainted; for they are handsome, with soft gray fur, large eyes, and bushy tails; and, moreover, no one can avoid remarking their extraordinary habit of carrying to their burrows everything bright, useless, and portable, from an empty cartridge case to a skinning knife. But he knows nothing of mice, shrew, pocket gophers, or weasels; and but little even of some larger mammals with very marked characteristics. Thus I have met but one or two plainsmen who knew anything of the curious plains ferret, that rather rare weasel-like animal, which plays the same part on the plains that the mink does by the edges of all our streams and brooks, and the tree-loving sable in the cold northern forests. The ferret makes its home in burrows, and by preference goes abroad at dawn and dusk, but sometimes even at mid-day. It is as blood-thirsty as the mink itself, and its life is one long ramble for prey, gophers, prairie-dogs, sage rabbits, jack-rabbits, snakes, and every kind of ground bird furnishing its food. I have known one to fairly depopulate a prairie-dog town, it being the arch foe of these little rodents, because of its insatiable blood lust and its capacity to follow them into their burrows. Once I found the bloody body and broken eggs of a poor prairie-hen which a ferret had evidently surprised on her nest. Another time one of my men was eye-witness to a more remarkable instance of the little animal's blood-thirsty ferocity. He was riding the range, and being attracted by a slight commotion in a clump of grass, he turned his horse thither to look, and to his astonishment found an antelope fawn at the last gasp, but still feebly struggling, in the grasp of a ferret, which had throttled it and was sucking its blood with hideous greediness. He avenged the murdered innocent by a dexterous blow with the knotted end of his lariat.

That mighty bird of rapine, the war eagle, which on the great plains and among the Rockies supplants the bald-headed eagle of better-watered regions, is another dangerous foe of the young antelope. It is even said that under exceptional circumstances eagles will assail a full grown prong-horn; and a neighboring ranchman informs me that he was once an eye-witness to such an attack. It was a bleak day in the late winter, and he was riding home across a wide dreary plateau, when he saw two eagles worrying and pouncing on a prong-buck—seemingly a yearling. It made a gallant fight. The eagles hovered over it with spread wings, now and then swooping down, their talons out-thrust, to strike at the head, or to try to settle on the loins. The antelope reared and struck with hoofs and horns like a goat; but its strength was failing rapidly, and doubtless it would have succumbed in the end had not the approach of the ranchman driven off the marauders.

I have likewise heard stories of eagles attacking badgers, foxes, bob-cats, and coyotes; but I am inclined to think all such cases exceptional. I have never myself seen an eagle assail anything bigger than a fawn, lamb, kid, or jack-rabbit. It also swoops at geese, sage fowl, and prairie fowl. On one occasion while riding over the range I witnessed an attack on a jack-rabbit. The eagle was soaring overhead, and espied the jack while the latter was crouched motionless. Instantly the great bird rushed down through the humming air, with closed wings; checked itself when some forty yards above the jack, hovered for a moment, and again fell like a bolt. Away went long-ears, running as only a frightened jack can; and after him the eagle, not with the arrowy rush of its descent from high air, but with eager, hurried flapping. In a short time it had nearly overtaken the fugitive, when the latter dodged sharply to one side, and the eagle overshot it precisely as a grayhound would have done, stopping itself by a powerful, setting motion of the great pinions. Twice this manœuvre was repeated; then the eagle made a quick rush, caught and overthrew the quarry before it could turn, and in another moment was sitting triumphant on the quivering body, the crooked talons driven deep into the soft, furry sides.

Once while hunting mountain sheep in the Bad Lands I killed an eagle on the wing with the rifle. I was walking beneath a cliff of gray clay, when the eagle sailed into view over the crest. As soon as he saw me he threw his wings aback, and for a moment before wheeling poised motionless, offering a nearly stationary target; so that my bullet grazed his shoulder, and down he came through the air, tumbling over and over. As he struck the ground he threw himself on his back, and fought against his death with the undaunted courage proper to his brave and cruel nature.

Indians greatly prize the feathers of this eagle. With them they make their striking and beautiful war bonnets, and bedeck the manes and tails of their spirited war ponies. Every year the Grosventres and Mandans from the Big Missouri come to the neighborhood of my ranch to hunt. Though not good marksmen they kill many whitetail deer, driving the bottoms for them in bands, on horseback; and they catch many eagles. Sometimes they take these alive by exposing a bait near which a hole is dug, where one of them lies hidden for days, with Indian patience, until an eagle lights on the bait and is noosed.

Even eagles are far less dangerous enemies to antelope than are wolves and coyotes. These beasts are always prowling round the bands, to snap up the sick or unwary; and in spring they revel in carnage of the kids and fawns. They are not swift enough to overtake the grown animals by sheer speed; but they are superior in endurance, and especially in winter, often run them down in fair chase. A prong-buck is a plucky little beast, and when cornered it often makes a gallant, though not a very effectual, fight.

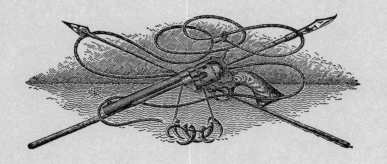

In Cowboy Land

A Bucking Bronco

The Fugitive

III
In Cowboy Land

Out on the frontier, and generally among those who spend their lives in, or on the borders of, the wilderness, life is reduced to its elemental conditions. The passions and emotions of these grim hunters of the mountains, and wild rough-riders of the plains, are simpler and stronger than those of people dwelling in more complicated states of society. As soon as the communities become settled and begin to grow with any rapidity, the American instinct for law asserts itself; but in the earlier stages each individual is obliged to be a law to himself and to guard his rights with a strong hand. Of course the transition periods are full of incongruities. Men have not yet adjusted their relations to morality and law with any niceness. They hold strongly by certain rude virtues, and on the other hand they quite fail to recognize even as shortcomings not a few traits that obtain scant mercy in older communities. Many of the desperadoes, the man-killers, and road-agents have good sides to their characters. Often they are people who, in

95

certain stages of civilization, do, or have done, good work, but who, when these stages have passed, find themselves surrounded by conditions which accentuate their worst qualities, and make their best qualities useless. The average desperado, for instance, has, after all, much the same standard of morals that the Norman nobles had in the days of the battle of Hastings, and, ethically and morally, he is decidedly in advance of the vikings, who were the ancestors of these same nobles—and to whom, by the way, he himself could doubtless trace a portion of his blood. If the transition from the wild lawlessness of life in the wilderness or on the border to a higher civilization were stretched out over a term of centuries, he and his descendants would doubtless accommodate themselves by degrees to the changing circumstances. But unfortunately in the far West the transition takes place with marvellous abruptness, and at an altogether unheard-of speed, and many a man's nature is unable to change with sufficient rapidity to allow him to harmonize with his environment. In consequence, unless he leaves for still wilder lands, he ends by getting hung instead of founding a family which would revere his name as that of a very capable, although not in all respects a conventionally moral, ancestor.

Most of the men with whom I was intimately thrown during my life on the frontier and in the wilderness were good fellows, hard-working, brave, resolute, and truthful. At times, of course, they were forced of necessity to do deeds which would seem startling to dwellers in cities and in old settled places; and though they waged a very stern and relentless warfare upon evil-doers whose misdeeds had immediate and tangible bad results, they showed a wide toleration of all save the most extreme classes of wrong, and were not given to inquiring too curiously into a strong man's past, or to criticising him over-harshly for a failure to discriminate in finer ethical questions. Moreover, not a few of the men with whom I came in contact—with some of whom my relations were very close and friendly—had at different times led rather tough careers. This fact was accepted by them and by their companions as a fact, and nothing more. There were certain offences, such as rape, the robbery of a friend, or murder under circumstances of cowardice and treachery, which were never forgiven; but the fact that when the country was wild a young fellow had gone on the road—that is, become a highwayman, or had been chief of a gang of desperadoes, horse-thieves, and cattle-killers, was scarcely held to weigh against him, being treated as a regrettable, but certainly not shameful, trait of youth. He was regarded by his neighbors with the same kindly tolerance which respectable mediæval Scotch borderers doubtless extended to their wilder young men who would persist in raiding English cattle even in time of peace.

Of course if these men were asked outright as to their stories they would have refused to tell them or else would have lied about them; but when they had grown to regard a man as a friend and companion they would often recount various incidents of their past lives with perfect frankness, and as they combined in a very curious degree both a decided sense of humor, and a failure to appreciate that there was anything especially remarkable in what they related, their tales were always entertaining.

Early one spring, now nearly ten years ago, I was out hunting some lost horses. They had strayed from the range three months before, and we had in a roundabout way heard that they were ranging near some broken country, where a man named Brophy had a ranch, nearly fifty miles from my own. When I started thither the weather was warm, but the second day out it grew colder and a heavy snowstorm came on. Fortunately I was able to reach the ranch all right, finding there one of the sons of a Little Beaver ranchman, and a young cowpuncher belonging to a Texas outfit, whom I knew very well. After putting my horse into the corral and throwing him down some hay I strode into the low hut, made partly of turf and partly of cottonwood logs, and speedily warmed myself before the fire. We had a good warm supper, of bread, potatoes, fried venison, and tea. My two companions grew very sociable and began to talk freely over their pipes. There were two bunks one above the other. I climbed into the upper, leaving my friends, who occupied the lower, sitting together on a bench recounting different incidents in the careers of themselves and their cronies during the winter that had just passed. Soon one of them asked the other what had become of a certain horse, a noted cutting pony, which I had myself noticed the preceding fall. The question aroused

the other to the memory of a wrong which still
rankled, and he began (I alter one or two of the
proper names):

"Why, that was the pony that got stole.
I had been workin' him on rough ground
when I was out with the Three Bar outfit
and he went tender forward,
so I turned him loose by the Lazy B ranch,
and when I come back to git him
there wasn't anybody at the ranch
and I couldn't find him.
The sheep-man who lives about two miles west,
under Red Clay butte,
told me he seen a fellow in a wolf-skin coat,
ridin' a pinto bronco, with white eyes,
leadin' that pony of mine just two days before;
and I hunted round till I hit his trail
and then I followed
to where I'd reckoned he was headin' for—
the Short Pine Hills.
When I got there
a rancher told me he had seen the man
pass on towards Cedartown,
and sure enough
when I struck Cedartown
I found he lived there in a 'dobe house
just outside the town.
There was a boom on the town
and it looked pretty slick.
There was two hotels and I went into the first,
and I says,
'Where's the justice of the peace?'
says I to the bartender.

"'There ain't no justice of the peace,'
   says he,
   'the justice of the peace got shot.'

"'Well, where's the constable?'
   says I.

"'Why, it was him that shot the justice of the peace!'
   says he;
   'he's skipped the country with a bunch of horses.'

"'Well, ain't there no officer of the law
   left in this town?'
   says I.

"'Why, of course,'
   says he,
   'there's a probate judge;
   he is over tendin' bar at the Last Chance Hotel.'

   "So I went over to the Last Chance Hotel
   and I walked in there.
   'Mornin,'' says I.

"'Mornin,'' says he.

"'You're the probate judge?' says I.

"'That's what I am,' says he.
   'What do you want?' says he.

"'I want justice,' says I.

"'What kind of justice do you want?' says he.
   'What's it for?'

"'It's for stealin' a horse,' says I.

"'Then by God you'll git it,' says he.
  'Who stole the horse?' says he.

"'It is a man that lives in a 'dobe house,
  just outside the town there,' says I.

"'Well, where do you come from yourself?' said he.

"'From Medory,' said I.

  "With that he lost interest and settled kind o' back,
    and says he,
  'There wont no Cedartown jury
  hang a Cedartown man
  for stealin' a Medory man's horse,'
    said he.

"'Well, what am I to do about my horse?'
    says I.

"'Do? says he;
  'well, you know where the man lives,
  don't you?'
    says he;
  'then sit up outside his house tonight
  and shoot him when he comes in,'
    says he,
  'and skip out with the horse.'

"'All right,'
    says I,
  'that is what I'll do,'
  and I walked off.

"So I went off to his house
and I laid down behind some sage-brushes
to wait for him.
He was not at home,
but I could see his wife
movin' about inside now and then,
and I waited and waited,
and it growed darker,
and I begun to say to myself,
'Now here you are lyin' out
to shoot this man when he come home;
and it's gettin' dark,
and you don't know him,
and if you do shoot the next man
that comes into that house,
like as not
it won't be the fellow you're after at all,
but some perfectly innocent man
a-comin' there after the other man's wife!'

"So I up and saddled the bronc'
and lit out for home,"
concluded the narrator
with the air of one justly proud
of his own self-abnegating virtue.

The "town" where the judge above-mentioned
dwelt was one of those squalid, pretentiously
named little clusters of makeshift dwellings which
on the edge of the wild country spring up with the
rapid growth of mushrooms, and are often no
longer lived. In their earlier stages these towns are
frequently built entirely of canvas, and are subject
to grotesque calamities. When the territory

purchased from the Sioux, in the Dakotas, a couple of years ago, was thrown open to settlement, there was a furious inrush of men on horseback and in wagons, and various ambitious cities sprang up overnight. The new settlers were all under the influence of that curious craze which causes every true westerner to put unlimited faith in the unknown and untried; many had left all they had in a far better farming country, because they were true to their immemorial belief that, wherever they were, their luck would be better if they went somewhere else. They were always on the move, and headed for the vague beyond. As miners see visions of all the famous mines of history in each new camp, so these would-be city founders saw future St. Pauls and Omahas in every forlorn group of tents pitched by some muddy stream in a desert of gumbo and sage-brush; and they named both the towns and the canvas buildings in accordance with their bright hopes for the morrow, rather than with reference to the mean facts of the day. One of these towns, which when twenty-four hours old boasted of six saloons, a "court-house," and an "opera house," was overwhelmed by early disaster. The third day of its life a whirlwind came along and took off the opera house and half the saloons; and the following evening lawless men nearly finished the work of the elements. The raiders of a huge trail-outfit from Texas, to their glad surprise discovered the town and abandoned themselves to a night of roaring and lethal carousal. Next morning the city authorities were lamenting, with oaths of bitter rage, that "them hell-and-twenty Flying A cowpunchers had cut the court-house up into pants." It was true. The cowboys were in need of shaps, and with an admirable mixture of adventurousness, frugality, and ready adaptability to circumstances, had made substitutes therefor in the shape of canvas overalls, cut from the roof and walls of the shaky temple of justice.

One of my valued friends in the mountains, and one of the best hunters with whom I ever travelled, was a man who had a peculiarly light-hearted way of looking at conventional social obligations. Though in some ways a true backwoods Donatello, he was a man of much shrewdness and of great courage and resolution. Moreover, he possessed what only a few men do possess, the capacity to tell the truth. He saw facts as they were, and could tell them as they were, and he never told an untruth unless for very weighty reasons. He was pre-eminently a philosopher, of a happy, sceptical turn of mind. He had no prejudices. He never looked down, as so many hard characters do upon a person possessing a different code of ethics. His attitude was one of broad, genial tolerance. He saw nothing out of the way in the fact that he had himself been a road-agent, a professional gambler, and a desperado at different stages of his career. On the other hand, he did not in the least hold it against any one that he had always acted within the law. At the time that I knew him he had become a man of some substance, and naturally a staunch upholder of the existing order of things. But while he never boasted of his past deeds, he never apologized for them, and evidently would

have been quite as incapable of understanding that
they needed an apology as he would have been
incapable of being guilty of mere vulgar boastful-
ness. He did not often allude to his past career at
all. When he did, he recited its incidents perfectly
naturally and simply, as events, without any
reference to or regard for their ethical significance.
It was this quality which made him at times a
specially pleasant companion, and always an
agreeable narrator. The point of his story, or what
seemed to him the point, was rarely that which
struck me. It was the incidental sidelights the story
threw upon his own nature and the somewhat
lurid surroundings amid which he had moved.

On one occasion when we were out together we
killed a bear, and after skinning it, took a bath in
a lake. I noticed he had a scar on the side of his
foot and asked him how he got it, to which he
responded, with indifference:

"Oh, that?
Why, a man shootin' at me to make me dance,
that was all."

I expressed some curiosity in the matter,
and he went on:

"Well, the way of it was this:
It was when
I was keeping a saloon in New Mexico,
and there was a man there by the name of Fowler,
and there was a reward on him
of three thousand dollars..."

"Put on him by the State?"

"No, put on by his wife,"
  said my friend;
"and there was this..."

"Hold on,"
  I interrupted;
"put on by his wife did you say?"

"Yes, by his wife.
  Him and her had been keepin' a faro bank,
  you see,
  and they quarrelled about it,
  so she just put a reward on him, and so..."

"Excuse me," I said
"but do you mean to say
  that this reward was put on publicly?"
  to which my friend answered,
  with an air of gentlemanly boredom
  at being interrupted
  to gratify my thirst for irrelevant detail:

"Oh, no, not publicly.
  She just mentioned it
  to six or eight intimate personal friends."

"Go on,"
  I responded, somewhat overcome
  by this instance of the primitive simplicity
  with which New Mexican matrimonial disputes
  were managed,
  and he continued:

"Well, two men come ridin' in to see me
to borrow my guns.
My guns was Colt's self-cockers.
It was a new thing then,
and they was the only ones in town.
These come to me, and
'Simpson,' says they,
'we want to borrow your guns;
we are goin' to kill Fowler.'

"'Hold on for a moment,'
said I,
'I am willin' to lend you them guns,
but I ain't goin' to know
what you 'r' goin' to do with them,
no sir;
but of course you can have the guns.'"
Here my friend's face lightened pleasantly,
and he continued:

"Well, you may easily believe
I felt surprised next day
when Fowler come ridin' in,
and, says he,
'Simpson, here's your guns!'
He had shot them two men!
'Well, Fowler,'
says I,
if I had known them men was after you,
I'd never have let them have them guns nohow.'
says I.
That wasn't true,
for I did know it,
but there was no cause to tell him that."

I murmured my approval of such prudence,
and Simpson continued,
his eyes gradually brightening
with the light of agreeable reminiscence:

"Well, they up and they took Fowler
before the justice of the peace.
The justice of the peace was a Turk."

"Now, Simpson, what do you mean by that?"
I interrupted.

"Well, he come from Turkey," said Simpson,
and I again sank back wondering briefly
what particular variety of Mediterranean outcast
had drifted down to New Mexico
to be made a justice of the peace.
Simpson laughed and continued.

"That Fowler was a funny fellow.
The Turk, he committed Fowler,
and Fowler, he riz up and knocked him down
and tromped all over him
and made him let him go!"

"That was an appeal to a higher law,"
I observed.
Simpson assented cheerily, and continued:

"Well, that Turk,
he got nervous for fear
Fowler he was goin' to kill him,
and so he comes to me
and offers me twenty-five dollars a day
to protect him from Fowler;

and I went to Fowler, and
'Fowler,' says I,
'that Turk's offered me twenty-five dollars a day
to protect him from you.
Now, I ain't goin' to get shot
for no twenty-five dollars a day,
and if you are goin' to kill the Turk,
just say so and go and do it;
but if you ain't goin' to kill the Turk,
there's no reason why
I shouldn't earn that twenty-five dollars a day!'
and Fowler, says he,
'I ain't goin' to touch the Turk;
you just go right ahead and protect him.'"

So Simpson "protected" the Turk
from the imaginary danger of Fowler,
for about a week,
at twenty-five dollars a day.
Then one evening
he happened to go out and met Fowler.
"and," said he,
"the moment I saw him I knowed he felt mean,
for he begun to shoot at my feet,"
which certainly did seem
to offer presumptive evidence of meanness.
Simpson continued:

"I didn't have no gun,
so I just had to stand there and take it
until something distracted his attention,
and I went off home to get my gun and kill him,
but I wanted to do it perfectly lawful;
so I went up to the mayor
(he was playin' poker with one of the judges),

and says I to Him,
'Mr. Mayor,' says I,
'I am goin' to shoot Fowler.
And the mayor he riz out of his chair
and he took me by the hand,
and says he,
'Mr. Simpson, if you do I will stand by you';
and the judge, he says,
'I'll go on your bond.'"

Fortified by this cordial approval of the executive
and judicial branches of the government,
Mr. Simpson started on his quest. Meanwhile,
however, Fowler had cut up another prominent
citizen, and they already had him in jail. The
friends of law and order feeling some little distrust
as to the permanency of their own zeal for
righteousness, thought it best to settle the matter
before there was time for cooling, and accordingly,
headed by Simpson, the mayor, the judge, the
Turk, and other prominent citizens of the town,
they broke into the jail and hanged Fowler.
The point in the hanging which especially tickled
my friend's fancy, as he lingered over the
reminiscence, was one that was rather too ghastly
to appeal to our own sense of humor. In the
Turk's mind there still rankled the memory of
Fowler's very unprofessional conduct while
figuring before him as a criminal. Said Simpson,
with a merry twinkle of the eye:

"Do you know that Turk,
he was a right funny fellow too after all.

Just as the boys
were going to string up Fowler,
says he,
'Boys, stop; one moment, gentlemen,—
Mr. Fowler, good-by,'
and he blew a kiss to him!"

In the cow-country, and elsewhere on the wild
borderland between savagery and civilization, men
go quite as often by nicknames as by those to which
they are lawfully entitled. Half the cowboys and
hunters of my acquaintance are known by names
entirely unconnected with those they inherited or
received when they were christened. Occasionally
some would-be desperado or make-believe mighty
hunter tries to adopt what he deems a title suitable
to his prowess; but such an effort is never attempted
in really wild places, where it would be greeted
with huge derision; for all of these names that are
genuine are bestowed by outsiders, with small
regard to the wishes of the person named.
Ordinarily the name refers to some easily
recognizable accident of origin, occupation, or
aspect; as witness the innumerable Dutcheys,
Frencheys, Kentucks, Texas Jacks, Bronco Bills,
Bear Joes, Buckskins, Red Jims, and the like.
Sometimes it is apparently meaningless; one of my
cowpuncher friends is always called "Sliver" or
"Splinter"—why, I have no idea. At other times
some particular incident may give rise to the title: a
clean-looking cowboy formerly in my employ was
always known as "Muddy Bill," because he had once
been bucked off his horse into a mud hole.

The grewsome genesis of one such name is given in the following letter which I have just received from an old hunting-friend in the Rockies, who took a kindly interest in a frontier cabin which the Boone and Crockett Club was putting up at the Chicago World's Fair.

Feb 16th 1893; Der Sir:
I see in the newspapers that your club the Daniel Boon and Davey Crockit you Intend to erect a fruntier Cabin at the world's Far at Chicago to represent the erley Pianears of our country I would like to see you maik a success I have all my life been a fruntiersman and feel interested in your undertaking and I hoap you wile get a good assortment of relicks I want to maik one suggestion to you that is in regard to geting a good man and a genuine Mauntanner to take charg of your haus at Chicago I want to recommend a man for you to get it is Liver-eating Johnson that is the naim he is generally called he is an olde mauntneer and large and fine looking and one of the Best Story Tellers in the country and Very Polight genteel to every one he meets I wil tel you how he got that naim Liver-eating in a hard Fight with the Black Feet Indians thay Faught all day Johnson and a few Whites Faught a large Body of Indians all day after the fight Johnson cam in contact with a wounded Indian and Johnson was aut of ammunition and thay faught it out with thar Knives and Johnson got away with the Indian and in the fight cut the livver out of the Indian and said to the Boys did thay want any Liver to eat that is the way he got the naim of Liver-eating Johnson
Yours truly, etc., etc.

Frontiersmen are often as original in their theories
of life as in their names; and the originality
may take the form of wild savagery, of mere
uncouthness, or of an odd combination of genuine
humor with simple acceptance of facts as they are.

On one occasion I expressed some surprise at
learning that a certain Mrs. P. had suddenly
married, though her husband was alive and in jail
in a neighboring town; and received for answer:

"Well, you see,
old man Pete he skipped the country,
and left his widow behind him,
and so Bob Evans
he up and married her!"—
which was evidently felt
to be a proceeding
requiring no explanation whatever.

In the cow-country there is nothing more
refreshing than the light-hearted belief entertained
by the average man to the effect that any animal
which by main force has been saddled and ridden,
or harnessed and driven a couple of times, is a
"broke horse." My present foreman is firmly
wedded to this idea, as well as to its complement,
the belief that any animals with hoofs, before any
vehicle with wheels, can be driven across any
country. One summer on reaching the ranch
I was entertained with the usual accounts of the
adventures and misadventures which had befallen
my own men and my neighbors since I had been
out last. In the course of the conversation my
foreman remarked:

"We had a great time out here
about-six weeks ago.
There was a professor from Ann Arbor
came out with his wife to see the Bad Lands,
and they asked if we could rig them up a team,
and we said we guessed we could,
and Foley's boy and I did;
but it ran away with him and broke his leg!
He was here for a month.
I guess he didn't mind it though."

Of this I was less certain,
forlorn little Medora being a "busted" cow town,
concerning which I once heard
another of my men remark,
in reply to an inquisitive commercial traveller:

"How many people lives here?
Eleven—counting the chickens—
when they're all in town!"

My foreman continued:
"By George, there was something
that professor said afterwards
that made me feel hot.
I sent word up to him by Foley's boy
that seein' as how it had come out
we wouldn't charge him nothin' for the rig;
and that professor he answered
that he was glad we were showing him
some sign of consideration,
for he'd begun to believe
he'd fallen into a den of sharks.
and that we gave him a runaway team a purpose.

That made me hot,
calling that a runaway team.
Why, there was one of them horses
never *could* have run away before;
it hadn't never been druv but twice!
and the other horse
maybe had run away a few times,
but there was lots of times
he *hadn't* run away.
I esteemed that team
full as liable not to run away
as it was to run away,"
concluded my foreman,
evidently deeming this
as good a warranty of gentleness
as the most exacting could require.

The definition of good behavior on the frontier is
even more elastic for a saddle-horse than for a
team. Last spring one of the Three-Seven riders, a
magnificent horseman, was killed on the round-up
near Belfield, his horse bucking and falling on him.
"It was accounted a plumb gentle horse too," said my
informant, "only it sometimes sulked and acted a
little mean when it was cinched up behind." The
unfortunate rider did not know of this failing of
the "plumb gentle horse," and as soon as he was in
the saddle it threw itself over sideways with a
great bound, and he fell on his head, and never
spoke again.

Such accidents are too common in the wild country
to attract very much attention; the men accept them
with grim quiet, as inevitable in such lives as

theirs—lives that are harsh and narrow in their toil and their pleasure alike, and that are ever-bounded by an iron horizon of hazard and hardship. During the last year and a half three other men from the ranches in my immediate neighborhood have met their deaths in the course of their work. One, a trail boss of the OX, was drowned while swimming his herd across a swollen river. Another, one of the fancy ropers of the W Bar, was killed while roping cattle in a corral; his saddle turned, the rope twisted round him, he was pulled off, and was trampled to death by his own horse.

The fourth man, a cowpuncher named Hamilton, lost his life during the last week of October, 1891, in the first heavy snowstorm of the season. Yet he was a skilled plainsman, on ground he knew well, and just before straying himself, he successfully instructed two men who did not know the country how to get to camp. They were all three with the round-up, and were making a circle through the Bad Lands; the wagons had camped on the eastern edge of these Bad Lands, where they merge into the prairie, at the head of an old disused road, which led about due east from Little Missouri. It was a gray, lowering day, and as darkness came on Hamilton's horse played out, and he told his two companions not to wait, as it had begun to snow, but to keep on towards the north, skirting some particularly rough buttes, and as soon as they struck the road to turn to the right and follow it out to the prairie, where they would find camp; he particularly warned them to keep a sharp look-out, so as not to pass over the dim trail unawares in the dusk and the storm. They followed his advice, and reached camp safely; and after they had left him nobody ever again saw him alive. Evidently he himself, plodding northwards, passed over the road without seeing it in the gathering gloom; probably he struck it at some point where the ground was bad, and the dim trail in consequence disappeared entirely, as is the way with these prairie roads—making them landmarks to be used with caution. He must then have walked on and on, over rugged hills and across deep ravines, until his horse came to a standstill; he took off its saddle and picketed it to a dwarfed ash. Its frozen carcass was found, with the saddle near by, two months later. He now evidently recognized some landmark, and realized that he had passed the road, and was far to the north of the round-up wagons; but he was a resolute, self-confident man, and he determined to strike out for a line camp, which he knew lay about due east of him, two or three miles out on the prairie, on one of the head branches of Knife River. Night must have fallen by this time, and he missed the camp, probably passing it within less than a mile; but he did pass it, and with it all hopes of life, and walked wearily on to his doom, through the thick darkness and the driving snow. At last his strength failed, and he lay down in the tall grass of a little hollow. Five months later, in the early spring, the riders from the line camp found his body, resting face downwards, with the forehead on the folded arms.

Accidents of less degree are common. Men break their collar-bones, arms, or legs by falling when

riding at speed over dangerous ground, when
cutting cattle or trying to control a stampeded herd,
or by being thrown or rolled on by bucking or
rearing horses; or their horses, and on rare
occasions even they themselves, are gored by
fighting steers. Death by storm or in flood, death in
striving to master a wild and vicious horse, or in
handling maddened cattle, and too often death in
brutal conflict with one of his own fellows—any one
of these is the not unnatural end of the life of the
dweller on the plains or in the mountains.

But a few years ago other risks had to be run from
savage beasts, and from the Indians. Since I have
been ranching on the Little Missouri, two men
have been killed by bears in the neighborhood of
my range; and in the early years of my residence
there, several men living or travelling in the
country were slain by small war-parties of young
braves. All the old-time trappers and hunters
could tell stirring tales of their encounters
with Indians.

My friend, Tazewell Woody, was among the chief
actors in one of the most noteworthy adventures of
this kind. He was a very quiet man, and it was
exceedingly difficult to get him to talk over any of
his past experiences; but one day, when he was in
high good-humor with me for having made three
consecutive straight shots at elk, he became quite
communicative, and I was able to get him to tell
me one story which I had long wished to hear
from his lips, having already heard of it through
one of the other survivors of the incident.

When he found that I already knew a good deal old Woody told me the rest.

It was in the spring of 1875, and Woody and two friends were trapping on the Yellowstone. The Sioux were very bad at the time and had killed many prospectors, hunters, cowboys, and settlers; the whites retaliated whenever they got a chance, but, as always in Indian warfare, the sly, lurking, bloodthirsty savages inflicted much more loss than they suffered.

The three men, having a dozen horses with them, were camped by the river-side in a triangular patch of brush, shaped a good deal like a common flat-iron. On reaching camp they started to put out their traps; and when he came back in the evening Woody informed his companions that he had seen a great deal of Indian sign, and that he believed there were Sioux in the neighborhood. His companions both laughed at him, assuring him that they were not Sioux at all but friendly Crows, and that they would be in camp next morning; "and sure enough," said Woody, meditatively, "they *were* in camp next morning." By dawn one of the men went down the river to look at some of the traps, while Woody started out to where the horses were, the third man remaining in camp to get breakfast. Suddenly two shots were heard down the river, and in another moment a mounted Indian swept towards the horses. Woody fired, but missed him, and he drove off five while Woody, running forward, succeeded in herding the other seven into camp. Hardly had this been accomplished before the man who had gone down the river appeared, out of breath with his desperate run, having been surprised by several Indians, and just succeeding in making his escape by dodging from bush to bush, threatening his pursuers with his rifle.

These proved to be but the forerunners of a great war party, for when the sun rose the hills around seemed black with Sioux. Had they chosen to dash right in on the camp, running the risk of losing several of their men in the charge, they could of course have eaten up the three hunters in a minute; but such a charge is rarely practised by Indians, who, although they are admirable in defensive warfare, and even in certain kinds of offensive movements, and although from their skill in hiding they usually inflict much more loss than they suffer when matched against white troops, are yet very reluctant to make any movement where the advantage gained must be offset by considerable loss of life. The three men thought they were surely doomed, but being veteran frontiersmen and long inured to every kind of hardship and danger, they set to work with cool resolution to make as effective a defence as possible, to beat off their antagonists if they might, and if this proved impracticable, to sell their lives as dearly as they could. Having tethered the horses in a slight hollow, the only one which offered any protection, each man crept out to a point of the triangular brush patch and lay down to await events.

In a very short while the Indians began closing in on them, taking every advantage of cover, and then, both from their side of the river and from the opposite bank, opened a perfect fusillade, wasting their cartridges with a recklessness which Indians are apt to show when excited. The hunters could hear the hoarse commands of the chiefs, the war-whoops, and the taunts in broken English which some of the warriors hurled at them. Very soon all of their horses were killed, and the brush was fairly riddled by the incessant volleys; but the three men themselves, lying flat on the ground and well concealed, were not harmed. The more daring young warriors then began to creep toward the hunters, going stealthily from one piece of cover to the next; and now the whites in turn opened fire. They did not shoot recklessly, as did their foes, but coolly and quietly, endeavoring to make each shot tell. Said Woody: "I only fired seven times all day; I reckoned on getting meat every time I pulled trigger." They had an immense advantage over their enemies, in that whereas they lay still and entirely concealed, the Indians of course had to move from cover to cover in order to approach, and so had at times to expose themselves. When the whites fired at all they fired at a man, whether moving or motionless, whom they could clearly see, while the Indians could only shoot at the smoke, which imperfectly marked the position of their unseen foes. In consequence the assailants speedily found that it was a task of hopeless danger to try in such a manner to close in on three plains veterans, men of iron nerve and skilled in the use of the rifle. Yet some of the more daring crept up very close to the patch of brush, and one actually got inside it, and was killed among the bedding that lay by the smouldering camp-fire. The wounded and such of the dead as did not lie in too exposed positions were promptly taken away by their comrades; but seven bodies fell into the hands of the three hunters. I asked Woody how many he himself had killed. He said he could only be sure of two that he got; one he shot in the head as he peeped over a bush, and the other he shot through the smoke as he attempted to rush in. "My, how that Indian did yell," said Woody, retrospectively; "*he* was no great of a Stoic." After two or three hours of this deadly skirmishing, which resulted in nothing more serious to the whites than in two of them being slightly wounded, the Sioux became disheartened by the loss they were suffering and withdrew, confining themselves thereafter to a long range and harmless fusillade. When it was dark the three men crept out to the river bed and taking advantage of the pitchy night broke through the circle of their foes; they managed to reach the settlements without further molestation, having lost everything except their rifles.

For many years one of the most important of the wilderness dwellers was the West Point officer, and no man has played a greater part than he in the wild warfare which opened the regions beyond the Mississippi to white settlement. Since 1879, there has been but little regular Indian fighting in the North, though there have been one or two very tedious and wearisome campaigns waged against the Apaches in the South. Even in the North, however, there have been occasional uprisings which had to be quelled by the regular troops.

After my elk hunt in September, 1891, I came out through the Yellowstone Park, as I have elsewhere related, riding in company with a surveyor of the Burlington and Quincy railroad, who was just coming in from his summer's work. It was the first of October. There had been a heavy snow-storm and the snow was still falling. Riding a stout pony each, and leading another packed with our bedding, etc., we broke our way from the upper to the middle geyser basin. Here we found a troop of the 1st Cavalry camped, under the command of old friends of mine, Captain Frank Edwards and Lieutenant (now Captain) John Pitcher. They gave us hay for our horses and insisted upon our stopping to lunch, with the ready hospitality always shown by army officers. After lunch we began exchanging stories. My travelling companion, the surveyor, had that spring performed a feat of note, going through one of the canyons of the Big Horn for the first time. He went with an old mining inspector, the two of them dragging a cottonwood sledge over the ice. The walls of the canyon are so sheer and the water so rough that it can be descended only when the stream is frozen. However, after six days' labor and hardship the descent was accomplished; and the surveyor, in concluding, described his experience in going through the Crow Reservation.

This turned the conversation upon Indians, and it appeared that both of our hosts had been actors in Indian scrapes which had attracted my attention at the time they occurred, as they took place among tribes that I knew and in a country which I had sometime visited, either when hunting or when purchasing horses for the ranch. The first, which occurred to Captain Edwards, happened late in 1886, at the time when the Crow Medicine Chief, Sword-Bearer, announced himself as the Messiah of the Indian race, during one of the usual epidemics of ghost dancing. Sword-Bearer derived his name from always wearing a medicine sword—that is, a sabre painted red. He claimed to possess magic power, and, thanks to the performance of many dextrous feats of juggling, and the lucky outcome of certain prophecies, he deeply stirred the Indians, arousing the young warriors in particular to the highest pitch of excitement. They became sullen, began to paint, and armed themselves; and the agent and the settlers nearby grew so apprehensive that the troops were ordered to go to the reservation. A body of cavalry, including Captain Edwards' troop, was accordingly marched thither, and found the Crow warriors, mounted on their war ponies and dressed in their striking battle-garb, waiting on a hill.

The position of troops at the beginning of such an affair is always peculiarly difficult. The settlers round-about are sure to clamor bitterly against them, no matter what they do, on the ground that they are not thorough enough and are showing favor to the savages, while on the other hand, even if they fight purely in self-defence, a large number of worthy but weak-minded sentimentalists in the East are sure to shriek about their having brutally attacked the Indians. The war authorities always insist that they must not fire the first shot under any circumstances, and such were the orders at this time. The Crows on the hill-top showed a sullen and threatening front, and the troops advanced slowly towards them and then halted for a parley. Meanwhile a mass of black thunder-clouds gathering on the horizon threatened one of those cloudbursts of extreme severity and suddenness so characteristic of the plains country. While still trying to make arrangements for a parley, a horseman started out of the Crow ranks and galloped headlong down towards the troops. It was the medicine chief, Sword-Bearer. He was painted and in his battle-dress, wearing his war-bonnet of floating, trailing eagle feathers, while the plumes of the same bird were braided in the mane and tail of his fiery little horse. On he came at a gallop almost up to the troops and then began to circle around them, calling and singing and throwing his crimson sword into the air, catching it by the hilt as it fell. Twice he rode completely around the soldiers, who stood in uncertainty, not knowing what to make of his performance, and expressly forbidden to shoot at him. Then paying no further heed to them he rode back towards the Crows. It appears that he had told them that he would ride twice around the hostile force, and by his incantations would call down rain from heaven, which would make the hearts of the white men like water, so that they should go back to their homes. Sure enough, while the arrangements for the parley were still going forward, down came the cloudburst, drenching the command and making the ground on the hills in front nearly impassable; and before it dried a courier arrived with orders to the troops to go back to camp.

This fulfilment of Sword-Bearer's prophecy of course raised his reputation to the zenith and the young men of the tribe prepared for war, while the older chiefs, who more fully realized the power of the whites, still hung back. When the troops next appeared they came upon the entire Crow force, the women and children with their tepees being off to one side beyond a little stream while almost all the warriors of the tribe were gathered in front. Sword-Bearer started to repeat his former ride, to the intense irritation of the soldiers. Luckily, however, this time some of his young men could not be restrained. They too began to ride near the troops, and one of them was unable to refrain from firing on Captain Edwards' troop, which was in the van. This gave the soldiers their chance. They instantly responded with a volley, and Captain Edwards' troop charged. The fight lasted but a minute or two, for Sword-Bearer was struck by a bullet and fell, and as he had boasted himself invulnerable, and promised that his warriors should be invulnerable also if they would follow him, the hearts of the latter became as water and they broke in every direction. One of the amusing, though irritating, incidents of the affair was to see the plumed and painted warriors race headlong for the camp. plunge into the stream, wash off their war paint, and remove their feathers; in another moment they would be stolidly sitting on the ground, with their blankets over their shoulders, rising to greet the pursuing cavalry with unmoved composure and calm assurances that they had always been friendly and had much disapproved the conduct of the young bucks who had just been scattered on the field outside. It was much to the credit of the discipline of the army that no bloodshed followed the fight proper. The loss to the whites was small.

The other incident, related by Lieutenant Pitcher, took place in 1890, near Tongue River, in northern Wyoming. The command with which he was serving was camped near the Cheyenne Reservation. One day two young Cheyenne bucks met one of the government herders, and promptly killed him—in a sudden fit, half of ungovernable blood lust, half of mere ferocious light-heartedness. They then dragged his body into the brush and left it. The disappearance of the herder of course attracted attention, and a search was organized by the cavalry. At first the Indians stoutly denied all knowledge of the missing man; but when it became evident that the search party would shortly find him, two or three of the chiefs joined them, and piloted them to where the body lay; and acknowledged that he had been murdered by two of their band, though at first they refused to give their names. The commander of the post demanded that the murderers be given up. The chiefs said that they were very sorry, that this could not be done, but that they were willing to pay over any reasonable number of ponies to make amends for the death. This offer was of course promptly refused, and the commander notified them that if they did not surrender the murderers by a certain time he would hold the whole tribe responsible and would promptly move out and attack them. Upon this the chiefs, after holding full counsel with the tribe, told the commander that they had no power to surrender the murderers, but that the latter had said that sooner than see their tribe involved in a hopeless struggle they would of their own accord come in and meet the troops anywhere the latter chose to appoint, and die fighting. To this the commander responded: "All right; let them come into the agency in half an hour." The chiefs acquiesced, and withdrew.

Immediately the Indians sent mounted messengers at speed from camp to camp, summoning all their people to witness the act of fierce self-doom; and soon the entire tribe of Cheyennes, many of them having their faces blackened in token of mourning, moved down and took up a position on the hill-side close to the agency. At the appointed hour both young men appeared in their handsome war dress, galloped to the top of the hill near the encampment, and deliberately opened fire on the troops. The latter merely fired a few shots to keep the young desperadoes off, while Lieutenant Pitcher and a score of cavalrymen left camp to make a circle and drive them in; they did not wish to hurt them, but to capture and give them over to the Indians, so that the latter might be forced themselves to inflict the punishment. However, they were unable to accomplish their purpose; one of the young braves went straight at them, firing his rifle and wounding the horse of one of the cavalrymen, so that, simply in self-defence, the latter had to fire a volley, which laid low the assailant; the other, his horse having been shot, was killed in the brush, fighting to the last. All the while, from the moment the two doomed braves appeared until they fell, the Cheyennes on the hill-side had been steadily singing the death chant. When the young men had both died, and had thus averted the fate which their misdeeds would else have brought upon the tribe, the warriors took their bodies and bore them away for burial honors, the soldiers looking on in silence. Where the slain men were buried the whites never knew; but all that night they listened to the dismal wailing of the dirges with which the tribesmen celebrated their gloomy funeral rites.

Frontiersmen are not, as a rule, apt to be very superstitious. They lead lives too hard and practical, and have too little imagination in things spiritual and supernatural. I have heard but few ghost stories while living on the frontier, and these few were of a perfectly commonplace and conventional type.

But I once listened to a goblin story which rather impressed me. It was told by a grisled, weather-beaten old mountain hunter, named Bauman, who was born and had passed all his life on the frontier. He must have believed what he said, for he could hardly repress a shudder at certain points of the tale; but he was of German ancestry, and in childhood had doubtless been saturated with all kinds of ghost and goblin lore, so that many fearsome superstitions were latent in his mind;

besides, he knew well the stories told by the Indian medicine men in their winter camps, of the snow-walkers, and the spectres, and the formless evil beings that haunt the forest depths, and dog and waylay the lonely wanderer who after nightfall passes through the regions where they lurk; and it may be that when overcome by the horror of the fate that befell his friend, and when oppressed by the awful dread of the unknown, he grew to attribute, both at the time and still more in remembrance, weird and elfin traits to what was merely some abnormally wicked and cunning wild beast; but whether this was so or not, no man can say.

When the event occurred Bauman was still a young man, and was trapping with a partner among the mountains dividing the forks of the Salmon from the head of Wisdom River. Not having had much luck, he and his partner determined to go up into a particularly wild and lonely pass through which ran a small stream said to contain many beaver. The pass had an evil reputation because the year before a solitary hunter who had wandered into it was there slain, seemingly by a wild beast, the half-eaten remains being afterwards found by some mining prospectors who had passed his camp only the night before.

The memory of this event, however, weighed very lightly with the two trappers, who were as adventurous and hardy as others of their kind. They took their two lean mountain ponies to the foot of the pass, where they left them in an open beaver meadow, the rocky timber-clad ground being from thence onwards impracticable for horses. They then struck out on foot through the vast, gloomy forest, and in about four hours reached a little open glade where they concluded to camp, as signs of game were plenty.

There was still an hour or two of daylight left, and after building a brush lean-to and throwing down and opening their packs, they started up stream. The country was very dense and hard to travel through, as there was much down timber, although here and there the sombre woodland was broken by small glades of mountain grass.

At dusk they again reached camp. The glade in which it was pitched was not many yards wide, the tall, close-set pines and firs rising round it like a wall. On one side was a little stream, beyond which rose the steep mountain-slopes, covered with the unbroken growth of the evergreen forest.

They were surprised to find that during their short absence something, apparently a bear, had visited camp, and had rummaged about among their things, scattering the contents of their packs, and in sheer wantonness destroying their lean-to. The footprints of the beast were quite plain, but at first they paid no particular heed to them, busying themselves with rebuilding the lean-to, laying out their beds and stores, and lighting the fire.

While Bauman was making ready supper, it being already dark, his companion began to examine the tracks more closely, and soon took a brand from the fire to follow them up, where the intruder had walked along a game trail after leaving the camp. When the brand flickered out, he returned and took another, repeating his inspection of the footprints very closely. Coming back to the fire, he stood by it a minute or two, peering out into the darkness, and suddenly remarked: "Bauman, that bear has been walking on two legs." Bauman laughed at this, but his partner insisted that he was right, and upon again examining the tracks with a torch, they certainly did seem to be made by but two paws, or feet. However, it was too dark to make sure. After discussing whether the footprints could possibly be those of a human being, and coming to the conclusion that they could not be, the two men rolled up in their blankets, and went to sleep under the lean-to.

At midnight Bauman was awakened by some noise, and sat up in his blankets. As he did so his nostrils were struck by a strong, wild-beast odor, and he caught the loom of a great body in the darkness at the mouth of the lean-to. Grasping his rifle, he fired at the vague, threatening shadow, but must have missed, for immediately afterwards he heard the smashing of the underwood as the thing, whatever it was, rushed off into the impenetrable blackness of the forest and the night.

After this the two men slept but little, sitting up by the rekindled fire, but they heard nothing more. In the morning they started out to look at the few traps they had set the previous evening and to put out new ones. By an unspoken agreement they kept together all day, and returned to camp towards evening.

On nearing it they saw, hardly to their astonishment, that the lean-to had been again torn down. The visitor of the preceding day had returned, and in wanton malice had tossed about their camp kit and bedding, and destroyed the shanty. The ground was marked up by its tracks, and on leaving the camp it had gone along the soft earth by the brook, where the footprints were as plain as if on snow, and, after a careful scrutiny of the trail, it certainly did seem as if, whatever the thing was, it had walked off on but two legs.

The men, thoroughly uneasy, gathered a great heap of dead logs, and kept up a roaring fire throughout the night, one or the other sitting on guard most of the time. About midnight the thing came down through the forest opposite, across the brook, and stayed there on the hill-side for nearly an hour. They could hear the branches crackle as it moved about, and several times it uttered a harsh, grating, long-drawn moan, a peculiarly sinister sound. Yet it did not venture near the fire.

In the morning the two trappers, after discussing the strange events of the last thirty-six hours, decided that they would shoulder their packs and leave the valley that afternoon. They were the more ready to do this because in spite of seeing a good deal of game sign they had caught very little fur. However, it was necessary first to go along the line of their traps and gather them, and this they started out to do.

All the morning they kept together, picking up trap after trap, each one empty. On first leaving camp they had the disagreeable sensation of being followed. In the dense spruce thickets they occasionally heard a branch snap after they had passed; and now and then there were slight rustling noises among the small pines to one side of them.

At noon they were back within a couple of miles of camp. In the high, bright sunlight their fears seemed absurd to the two armed men, accustomed as they were, through long years of lonely wandering in the wilderness to face every kind of danger from man, brute, or element. There were still three beaver traps to collect from a little pond in a wide ravine near by. Bauman volunteered to gather these and bring them in, while his companion went ahead to camp and made ready the packs.

On reaching the pond Bauman found three beaver in the traps, one of which had been pulled loose and carried into a beaver house. He took several hours in securing and preparing the beaver, and when he started homewards he marked with some uneasiness how low the sun was getting. As he hurried towards camp, under the tall trees, the silence and desolation of the forest weighed on him. His feet made no sound on the pine needles, and the slanting sun rays, striking through among the straight trunks, made a gray twilight in which objects at a distance glimmered indistinctly. There was nothing to break the ghostly stillness which, when there is no breeze, always broods over these sombre primeval forests.

At last he came to the edge of the little glade where the camp lay, and shouted as he approached it, but got no answer. The camp fire had gone out, though the thin blue smoke was still curling upwards. Near it lay the packs, wrapped and arranged. At first Bauman could see nobody; nor did he receive an answer to his call. Stepping forward he again shouted, and as he did so his eye fell on the body of his friend, stretched beside the trunk of a great fallen spruce. Rushing towards it the horrified trapper found that the body was still warm, but that the neck was broken, while there were four great fang marks in the throat.

The footprints of the unknown beast-creature, printed deep in the soft soil, told the whole story.

The unfortunate man, having finished his packing, had sat down on the spruce log with his face to the fire, and his back to the dense woods, to wait for his companion. While thus waiting, his monstrous assailant, which must have been lurking nearby in the woods, waiting for a chance to catch one of the adventurers unprepared, came silently up from behind, walking with long, noiseless steps, and seemingly still on two legs. Evidently unheard, it reached the man, and broke his neck by wrenching his head back with its forepaws, while it buried its teeth in his throat. It had not eaten the body, but apparently had romped and gambolled round it in uncouth, ferocious glee, occasionally rolling over and over it; and had then fled back into the soundless depths of the woods.

Bauman, utterly unnerved, and believing that the creature with which he had to deal was something either half human or half devil, some great goblin-beast, abandoned everything but his rifle and struck off at speed down the pass, not halting until he reached the beaver meadows where the hobbled ponies were still grazing. Mounting, he rode onwards through the night, until far beyond the reach of pursuit.

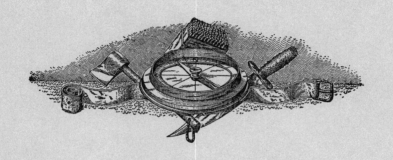

Hunting from the Ranch: The Blacktail Deer

Stalking Goats

A Deep Ford

IV
Hunting from the Ranch:
The Blacktail Deer

No life can be pleasanter than life during the
months of fall on a ranch in the northern cattle
country. The weather is cool; in the evenings and on
the rare rainy days we are glad to sit by the great
fireplace, with its roaring cottonwood logs. But on
most days not a cloud dims the serene splendor of
the sky; and the fresh pure air is clear with the
wonderful clearness of the high plains. We are in
the saddle from morning to night.

The long, low, roomy ranch house, of clean hewed
logs, is as comfortable as it is bare and plain.
We fare simply but well; for the wife of my
foreman makes excellent bread and cake, and
there are plenty of potatoes, grown in the forlorn
little garden-patch on the bottom. We also have
jellies and jams, made from wild plums and
buffalo berries; and all the milk we can drink.
For meat we depend on our rifles; and, with an
occasional interlude of ducks or prairie chickens,
the mainstay of each meal is venison, roasted,
broiled, or fried.

Sometimes we shoot the deer when we happen on them while about our ordinary business,—indeed throughout the time that I have lived on the ranch, very many of the deer and antelope I killed were thus obtained. Of course while doing the actual round-up work it is impossible to attend to anything else; but we generally carry rifles while riding after the saddle band in the early morning, while visiting the line camps, or while in the saddle among the cattle on the range; and get many a shot in this fashion.

In the fall of 1890 some friends came to my ranch; and one day we took them to see a round-up. The ox, a Texan steer-outfit, had sent a couple of wagons to work down the river, after beef cattle, and one of my men had gone along to gather any of my own scattered steers that were ready for shipping, and to brand the late calves. There were perhaps a dozen riders with the wagons; and they were camped for the day on a big bottom where Blacktail and Whitetail creeks open into the river, several miles below my ranch.

At dawn one of the men rode off to bring in the saddle band. The rest of us were up by sunrise; and as we stood on the verandah under the shimmering cottonwood trees, revelling in the blue of the cloudless sky, and drinking in the cool air before going to breakfast, we saw the motley-colored string of ponies file down from the opposite bank of the river, and splash across the broad, shallow ford in front of the ranch house. Cantering and trotting the band swept towards the high, round horse-corral, in the open glade to the rear of the house. Guided by the jutting wing which stuck out at right angles, they entered the open gate, which was promptly closed by the cowboy who had driven them in.

After breakfast we strolled over to the corral, with our lariats, and, standing by the snubbing-post in the middle, roped the horses we wished for the party—some that were gentle, and others that were not. Then every man saddled his horse; and at the moment of mounting for the start there was, as always, a thrill of mild excitement, each rider hoping that his own horse would not buck, and that his neighbor's would. I had no young horses on the ranch at the time; but a number of the older ones still possessed some of the least amiable traits of their youth.

Once in the saddle we rode off down river, along the bottoms, crossing the stream again and again. We went in Indian file, as is necessary among the trees and in broken ground, following the cattle-trails—which themselves had replaced or broadened the game paths that alone crossed the plateaus and bottoms when my ranch house was first built. Now we crossed open reaches of coarse grass, thinly sprinkled with large, brittle cottonwood trees, their branches torn and splintered; now we wound our way through a dense jungle where the gray, thorny buffalo bushes, spangled with brilliant red berry clusters, choked the spaces between the thick-growing box-alders; and again the sure-footed ponies scrambled down one cut bank and up another, through seemingly impossible rifts, or with gingerly footsteps trod a path which cut the side of a butte or overhung a bluff. Sometimes we racked, or shacked along at the fox trot which is the cow-pony's ordinary gait; and sometimes we loped or galloped and ran.

At last we came to the ford beyond which the riders of the round-up had made their camp. In the bygone days of the elk and buffalo, when our branded cattle were first driven thus far north, this ford had been dangerous from quicksand; but the cattle, ever crossing and re-crossing, had trodden down and settled the sand, and had found out the firm places; so that it was now easy to get over.

Close beyond the trees on the farther bank stood the two round-up wagons; near by was the cook's fire, in a trench, so that it might not spread; the bedding of the riders and horse-wranglers lay scattered about, each roll of blankets wrapped and corded in a stout canvas sheet. The cook was busy about the fire; the night-wrangler was snatching an hour or two's sleep under one of the wagons. Half a mile away, on the plain of sage brush and long grass, the day-wrangler was guarding the grazing or resting horse herd, of over a hundred head. Still farther distant, at the mouth of a ravine, was the day-herd of cattle, two or three cowboys watching it as they lolled drowsily in their saddles. The other riders were off on circles to bring in cattle to the round-up; they were expected every moment.

With the ready hospitality always shown in a

cow-camp we were pressed to alight and take dinner, or at least a lunch; and accordingly we jumped off our horses and sat down. Our tin plates were soon heaped with fresh beef, bread, tomatoes, rice, and potatoes, all very good; for the tall, bearded, scrawny cook knew his work, and the OX outfit always fed its men well,—and saw that they worked well too.

Before noon the circle riders began to appear on the plain, coming out of the ravines, and scrambling down the steep hills, singly or in twos and threes. They herded before them bunches of cattle, of varying size; these were driven together and left in charge of a couple of cow-punchers. The other men rode to the wagon to get a hasty dinner—lithe, sinewy fellows, with weather-roughened faces and fearless eyes; their broad felt hats flapped as they galloped, and their spurs and bridle chains jingled. They rode well, with long stirrups, sitting straight in the deep stock saddles, and their wiry ponies showed no signs of fatigue from the long morning's ride.

The horse-wrangler soon drove the saddle band to the wagons, where it was caught in a quickly improvised rope-corral. The men roped fresh horses, fitted for the cutting-work round the herd, with its attendant furious galloping and flash-like turning and twisting. In a few minutes all were in the saddle again and riding towards the cattle.

Then began that scene of excitement and turmoil, and seeming confusion, but real method and orderliness, so familiar to all who have engaged in stock-growing on the great plains. The riders gathered in a wide ring round the herd of uneasy cattle, and a couple of men rode into their midst to cut out the beef steers and the cows that were followed by unbranded calves. As soon as the animal was picked out the cowboy began to drive it slowly towards the outside of the herd, and when it was near the edge he suddenly raced it into the open. The beast would then start at full speed and try to double back among its fellows; while the trained cow-pony followed like a shadow, heading it off at every turn. The riders round that part of the herd opened out and the chosen animal was speedily hurried off to some spot a few hundred yards distant, where it was left under charge of another cowboy. The latter at first had his hands full in preventing his charge from rejoining the herd; for cattle dread nothing so much as being separated from their comrades. However, as soon as two or three others were driven out, enough to form a little bunch, it became a much easier matter to hold the"cut"as it is called. The cows and calves were put in one place, the beeves in another; the latter were afterwards run into the day-herd.

Meanwhile from time to time some clean-limbed young steer or heifer, able to run like an antelope and double like a jack-rabbit, tried to break out of the herd that was being worked, when the nearest cowboy hurried in pursuit at top speed and brought it back, after a headlong, break-neck race, in which no heed was paid to brush, fallen timber, prairie-dog holes, or cut banks. The dust rose in little

whirling clouds, and through it dashed bolting
cattle and galloping cowboys, hither and thither,
while the air was filled with the shouts and laughter
of the men, and the bellowing of the herd.

As soon as the herd was worked it was turned loose,
while the cows and calves were driven over to a
large corral, where the branding was done.
A fire was speedily kindled, and in it were laid the
branding irons of the different outfits represented
on the round-up. Then two of the best ropers rode
into the corral and began to rope the calves, round
the hind legs by preference, but sometimes round
the head. The other men dismounted to "wrestle"
and brand them. Once roped, the calf, bawling and
struggling, was swiftly dragged near the fire,
where one or two of the calf-wrestlers grappled
with and threw the kicking, plunging little beast,
and held it while it was branded. If the calf was
large the wrestlers had hard work; and one or two
young maverick bulls—that is, unbranded yearling
bulls, which had been passed by in the round-ups
of the preceding year—fought viciously, bellowing
and charging, and driving some of the men up the
sides of the corral, to the boisterous delight of
the others.

After watching the work for a little while we left
and rode homewards. Instead of going along the
river bottoms we struck back over the buttes.
From time to time we came out on some sharp
bluff overlooking the river. From these points of
vantage we could see for several miles up and down
the valley of the Little Missouri. The level bottoms

were walled in by rows of sheer cliffs, and steep, grassy slopes. These bluff lines were from a quarter of a mile to a mile apart; they did not run straight, but in a succession of curves, so as to look like the halves of many amphitheatres. Between them the river swept in great bends from side to side; the wide bed, brimful during the time of freshets, now held but a thin stream of water. Some of the bottoms were covered only with grass and sage brush; others with a dense jungle of trees; while yet others looked like parks, the cottonwoods growing in curved lines or in clumps scattered here and there.

On our way we came across a bunch of cattle, among which the sharp eyes of my foreman detected a maverick two-year-old heifer. He and one of the cowboys at once got down their ropes and rode after her; the rest of us first rounding up the bunch so as to give a fair start. After a sharp run one of the men, swinging his lariat round his head, got close up; in a second or two the noose settled round the heifer's neck, and as it became taut she was brought to with a jerk; immediately afterwards the other man made his throw and cleverly heeled her. In a trice the red heifer was stretched helpless on the ground, the two fierce little ponies, a pinto and a buckskin, keeping her down on their own account, tossing their heads and backing so that the ropes which led from the saddle-horns to her head and hind feet never slackened. Then we kindled a fire; one of the cinch rings was taken off to serve as a branding iron, and the heifer speedily became our property—for she was on our range.

When we reached the ranch it was still early, and after finishing dinner it lacked over an hour of sundown. Accordingly we went for another ride; and I carried my rifle. We started up a winding coulie which opened back of the ranch house; and after half an hour's canter clambered up the steep head-ravines, and emerged on a high ridge which went westward, straight as an arrow, to the main divide between the Little Missouri and the Big Beaver. Along this narrow, grassy crest we loped and galloped; we were so high that we could look far and wide over all the country round about. To the southward, across a dozen leagues of rolling and broken prairie, loomed Sentinel Butte, the chief landmark of all that region. Behind us, beyond the river, rose the weird chaos of Bad Lands which at this point lie for many miles east of the Little Missouri, Their fantastic outlines were marked against the sky as sharply as if cut with a knife; their grim and forbidding desolation warmed into wonderful beauty by the light of the dying sun. On our right, as we loped onwards, the land sunk away in smooth green-clad slopes and valleys; on our left it fell in sheer walls. Ahead of us the sun was sinking behind a mass of blood-red clouds; and on either hand the flushed skies were changing their tint to a hundred hues of opal and amethyst. Our tireless little horses sprang under us, thrilling with life; we were riding through a fairy world of beauty and color and limitless space and freedom.

Suddenly a short hundred yards in front three blacktail leaped out of a little glen and crossed our path, with the peculiar bounding gait of their kind. At once I sprang from my horse and, kneeling, fired at the last and largest of the three. My bullet sped too far back, but struck near the hip, and the crippled deer went slowly down a ravine. Running over a hillock to cut it off, I found it in some brush a few hundred yards beyond and finished it with a second ball. Quickly dressing it, I packed it on my horse, and trotted back leading him; an hour afterwards we saw through the waning light the quaint, home-like outlines of the ranch house.

After all, however, blacktail can only at times be picked up by chance in this way. More often it is needful to kill them by fair still-hunting, among the hills or wooded mountains where they delight to dwell. If hunted they speedily become wary. By choice they live in such broken country that it is difficult to pursue them with hounds; and they are by no means such water-loving animals as whitetail. On the other hand, the land in which they dwell is very favorable to the still-hunter who does not rely merely on stealth, but who can walk and shoot well. They do not go on the open prairie, and, if possible, they avoid deep forests, while, being good climbers, they like hills. In the mountains, therefore, they keep to what is called park country, where glades alternate with open groves. On the great plains they avoid both the heavily timbered river bottoms and the vast treeless stretches of level or rolling grass land; their chosen abode being the broken and hilly region, scantily wooded, which skirts almost every plains river and forms a belt, sometimes very narrow, sometimes

many miles in breadth, between the alluvial bottom
land and the prairies beyond. In these Bad Lands
dwarfed pines and cedars grow in the canyon-
like ravines and among the high steep hills;
there are also basins and winding coulies, filled
with brush and shrubbery and small elm or ash.
In all such places the blacktail loves to make
its home.

I have not often hunted blacktail in the mountains,
because while there I was generally after larger
game; but round my ranch I have killed more of
them than of any other game, and for me their
chase has always possessed a peculiar charm. We
hunt them in the loveliest season of the year, the fall
and early winter, when it is keen pleasure merely to
live out-of-doors. Sometimes we make a regular
trip, of several days' duration, taking the ranch
wagon, with or without a tent, to some rugged and
little disturbed spot where the deer are plenty;
perhaps returning with eight or ten carcasses, or
even more—enough to last a long while in cold
weather. We often make such trips while laying in
our winter supply of meat.

At other times we hunt directly from the ranch
house. We catch our horses overnight, and are in
the saddle for an all-day's hunt long before the first
streak of dawn, possibly not returning until some
hours after nightfall. The early morning and late
evening are the best time for hunting game, except
in regions where it is hardly ever molested, and
where in consequence it moves about more or less
throughout the day.

During the rut, which begins in September,
the deer are in constant motion, and are often found
in bands. The necks of the bucks swell and their
sides grow gaunt; they chase the does all night, and
their flesh becomes strong and stringy—far inferior
to that of the barren does and yearlings. The old
bucks then wage desperate conflicts with one
another, and bully their smaller brethren
unmercifully. Unlike the elk, the blacktail, like the
whitetail, are generally silent in the rutting season.
They occasionally grunt when fighting; and
once, on a fall evening, I heard two young bucks
barking in a ravine back of my ranch house, and
crept up and shot them; but this was a wholly
exceptional instance.

At this time I hunt on foot, only using the horse
to carry me to and from the hunting ground; for
while rutting, the deer, being restless, do not try to
escape observation by lying still, and on the other
hand are apt to wander about and so are easily seen
from a distance. When I have reached a favorable
place I picket my horse and go from vantage point
to vantage point, carefully scanning the hillsides,
ravines, and brush coulies from every spot that
affords a wide outlook. The quarry once seen it
may be a matter of hours, or only of minutes, to
approach it, accordingly as the wind and cover
are or are not favorable. The walks for many
miles over the hills, the exercise of constant
watchfulness, the excitement of the actual stalk,
and the still greater excitement of the shot, combine
to make still-hunting the blacktail, in the sharp fall
weather, one of the most attractive of hardy outdoor

sports. Then after the long, stumbling walk homewards, through the cool gloom of the late evening, comes the meal of smoking venison and milk and bread, and the sleepy rest, lying on the bear-skins, or sitting in the rocking chair before the roaring fire, while the icy wind moans outside.

Earlier in the season, while the does are still nursing the fawns, and until the bucks have cleaned the last vestiges of velvet from their antlers, the deer lie very close, and wander round as little as may be. In the spring and early summer, in the ranch country, we hunt big game very little, and then only antelope; because in hunting antelope there is no danger of killing aught but bucks. About the first of August we begin to hunt blacktail, but do not kill does until a month later—and then only when short of meat. In the early weeks of the deer season we frequently do even the actual hunting on horseback instead of on foot; because the deer at this time rarely appear in view, so as to afford chance for a stalk, and yet are reluctant to break cover until very closely approached. In consequence we keep on our horses, and so get over much more ground than on foot, beating through or beside all likely-looking cover, with the object of jumping the deer close by. Under such circumstances bucks sometimes lie until almost trodden on.

One afternoon in mid-August, when the ranch was entirely out of meat, I started with one of my cow-hands, Merrifield, to kill a deer. We were on a couple of stout, quiet ponies, accustomed to firing and to packing game. After riding a mile or two down the bottoms we left the river and struck off up a winding valley, which led back among the hills. In a short while we were in a blacktail country, and began to keep a sharp lookout for game, riding parallel to, but some little distance from, one another. The sun, beating down through the clear air, was very hot; the brown slopes of short grass, and still more the white clay walls of the Bad Lands, threw the heat rays in our faces. We skirted closely all likely-looking spots, such as the heavy brush-patches in the bottoms of the winding valleys, and the groves of ash and elm in the basins and pockets flanking the high plateaus; sometimes we followed a cattle trail which ran down the middle of a big washout, and again we rode along the brink of a deep cedar canyon. After a while we came to a coulie with a small muddy pool at its mouth; and round this pool there was much fresh deer sign. The coulie was but half a mile long, heading into and flanked by the spurs of some steep, bare hills. Its bottom, which was fifty yards or so across, was choked by a dense growth of brush, chiefly thorny bullberries, while the sides were formed by cut banks twelve or fifteen feet high. My companion rode up the middle, while I scrambled up one of the banks, and, dismounting, led my horse along its edge, that I might have a clear shot at whatever we roused. We went nearly to the head, and then the cowboy reined up and shouted to me that he "guessed there were no deer in the coulie." Instantly there was a smashing in the young trees midway between us, and I caught a glimpse of a blacktail buck speeding round a shoulder of the cut bank; and though I took a hurried shot I missed. However, another buck promptly jumped up from the same place; evidently the two had lain secure in their day-beds, shielded by the dense cover, while the cowboy rode by them, and had only risen when he halted and began to call to me across them. This second buck, a fine fellow with big antlers not yet clear of velvet, luckily ran up the opposite bank and I got a fair shot at him as he galloped broadside to me along the open hillside. When I fired he rolled over with a broken back. As we came up he bleated loudly, an unusual thing for a buck to do.

Now these two bucks must have heard us coming, but reckoned on our passing them by without seeing them; which we would have done had they not been startled when the cowboy halted and spoke. Later in the season they would probably not have let us approach them, but would have run as soon as they knew of our presence. Of course, however, even later in the season, a man may by chance stumble across a deer close by. I remember one occasion when my ranch partner, Robert Munro Ferguson, and I almost corralled an unlucky deer in a small washout.

It was October, and our meat supply unexpectedly gave out; on our ranch, as on most ranches, an occasional meat famine of three or four days intervenes between the periods of plenty. So Ferguson and I started together, to get venison, and at the end of two days' hard work, leaving the ranch by sunrise, riding to the hunting grounds and tramping steadily until dark, we succeeded. The weather was stormy and there were continual gusts of wind and of cold rain, sleet, or snow. We hunted through a large tract of rough and broken country, six or eight miles from the ranch. As often happens in such wild weather the deer were wild too; they were watchful and were on the move all the time. We saw a number, but either they ran off before we could get a shot, or if we did fire it was at such a distance or under such unfavorable circumstances that we missed. At last, as we were plodding drearily up a bare valley, the sodden mud caking round our shoes, we roused three deer from the mouth of a short washout but a few paces from us. Two bounded off; the third by mistake rushed into the washout, where he found himself in a regular trap and was promptly shot by my companion. We slung the carcass on a pole and carried it down to where we had left the horses; and then we loped homewards, bending to the cold slanting rain.

Although in places where it is much persecuted the blacktail is a shy and wary beast, the successful pursuit of which taxes to the uttermost the skill and energy of the hunter, yet, like the elk, if little molested it often shows astonishing tameness and even stupidity. In the Rockies I have sometimes come on blacktail within a very short distance, which would merely stare at me, then trot off a few yards, turn and stare again, and wait for several minutes before really taking alarm. What is much more extraordinary I have had the same thing happen to me in certain little hunted localities in the neighborhood of my ranch, even of recent years. In the fall of 1890 I was riding down a canyon-coulie with my foreman, Sylvane Ferris, and a young friend from Boston, when we almost rode over a barren blacktail doe. She only ran some fifty yards, round a corner of the coulie, and then turned and stood until we ran forward and killed her—for we were in need of fresh meat. One October, a couple of years before this, my cousin, West Roosevelt, and I took a trip with the wagon to a very wild and rugged country, some twenty miles from the ranch. We found that the deer had evidently been but little disturbed. One day while scrambling down a steep, brushy hill, leading my horse, I came close on a doe and fawn; they merely looked at me with curiosity for some time, and then sauntered slowly off, remaining within shot for at least five minutes. Fortunately we had plenty of meat at the time, and there was no necessity to harm the graceful creatures. A few days later we came on two bucks sunning themselves in the bottom of a valley. My companion killed one. The other was lying but a dozen rods off; yet it never moved, until several shots had been fired at the first. It was directly under me and in my anxiety to avoid overshooting, to my horror I committed the opposite fault, and away went the buck.

Every now and then any one will make most unaccountable misses. A few days after thus losing the buck I spent nearly twenty cartridges in butchering an unfortunate yearling, and only killed it at all because it became so bewildered by the firing that it hardly tried to escape. I never could tell why I used so many cartridges to such little purpose. During the next fortnight I killed seven deer without making a single miss, though some of the shots were rather difficult.

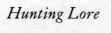

Hunting Lore

An Elk

In a Bog-Hole

V
Hunting Lore

It has been my good-luck to kill every kind of game
properly belonging to the United States: though
one beast which I never had a chance to slay, the
jaguar, from the torrid South, sometimes comes
just across the Rio Grande; nor have I ever hunted
the musk-ox and polar bear in the boreal wastes
where they dwell, surrounded by the frozen
desolation of the uttermost North.

I have never sought to make large bags, for a
hunter should not be a game butcher. It is always
lawful to kill dangerous or noxious animals, like
the bear, cougar, and wolf; but other game should
only be shot when there is need of the meat, or for
the sake of an unusually fine trophy. Killing a
reasonable number of bulls, bucks, or rams does no
harm whatever to the species; to slay half the males
of any kind of game would not stop the natural
increase, and they yield the best sport, and are the
legitimate objects of the chase. Cows, does, and
ewes, on the contrary, should only be killed (unless
barren) in case of necessity; during my last five

years' hunting I have killed but five—one by a mischance, and the other four for the table.

From its very nature, the life of the hunter is in most places evanescent; and when it has vanished there can be no real substitute in old settled countries. Shooting in a private game preserve is but a dismal parody; the manliest and healthiest features of the sport are lost with the change of conditions. We need, in the interest of the community at large, a rigid system of game laws rigidly enforced, and it is not only admissible, but one may almost say necessary, to establish, under the control of the State, great national forest reserves, which shall also be breeding grounds and nurseries for wild game; but I should much regret to see grow up in this country a system of large private game preserves, kept for the enjoyment of the very rich. One of the chief attractions of the life of the wilderness is its rugged and stalwart democracy; there every man stands for what he actually is, and can show himself to be.

There are, in different parts of our country, chances to try so many various kinds of hunting, with rifle or with horse and hound, that it is nearly impossible for one man to have experience of them all. There are many hunts I long hoped to take, but never did and never shall; they must be left for men with more time, or for those whose homes are nearer to the hunting grounds. I have never seen a grizzly roped by the riders of the plains, nor a black bear killed with the knife and hounds in the southern canebrakes; though at one time I had for many years a standing invitation to witness this last feat on a plantation in Arkansas. The friend who gave it, an old backwoods planter, at one time lost almost all his hogs by the numerous bears who infested his neighborhood. He took a grimly humorous revenge each fall by doing his winter killing among the bears instead of among the hogs they had slain; for as the cold weather approached he regularly proceeded to lay in a stock of bear-bacon, scouring the canebrakes in a series of systematic hunts, bringing the quarry to bay with the help of a big pack of hard-fighting mongrels, and then killing it with his long, broad-bladed bowie.

Again, I should like to make a trial at killing peccaries with the spear, whether on foot or on horseback, and with or without dogs. I should like much to repeat the experience of a friend who cruised northward through Bering Sea, shooting walrus and polar bear; and that of two other friends who travelled with dog-sleds to the Barren Grounds, in chase of the caribou, and of that last survivor of the Ice Age, the strange musk-ox. Once in a while it must be good sport to shoot alligators by torchlight in the everglades of Florida or the bayous of Louisiana.

If the big-game hunter, the lover of the rifle, has a taste for kindred field sports with rod and shotgun, many are his chances for pleasure, though perhaps of a less intense kind. The wild turkey really deserves a place beside the deer; to kill a wary old gobbler with the small-bore rifle, by fair still-hunting, is a triumph for the best sportsman. Swans, geese, and sandhill cranes likewise may sometimes be killed with the rifle; but more often all three, save perhaps the swan, must be shot over decoys. Then there is prairie-chicken shooting on the fertile grain prairies of the middle West, from Minnesota to Texas; and killing canvas-backs from behind blinds, with the help of that fearless swimmer, the Chesapeake Bay dog. In Californian mountains and valleys live the beautiful plumed quails, and who does not know their cousin bobwhite, the bird of the farm, with his cheery voice and friendly ways? For pure fun, nothing can surpass a night scramble through the woods after coon and possum.

The salmon, whether near Puget Sound or the St. Lawrence, is the royal fish; his only rival is the giant of the warm Gulf waters, the silver-mailed tarpon; while along the Atlantic coast the great striped bass likewise yields fine sport to the men of rod and reel. Every hunter of the mountains and the northern woods knows the many kinds of spotted trout; for the black bass he cares less; and least of all for the sluggish pickerel, and his big brother of the Great Lakes, the muskellunge.

Yet the sport yielded by rod and smooth-bore is really less closely kin to the strong pleasures so beloved by the hunter who trusts in horse and rifle than are certain other outdoor pastimes, of the rougher and hardier kind. Such a pastime is snow-shoeing, whether with webbed rackets, in the vast northern forests, or with skees, on the bare slopes of the Rockies. Such is mountaineering, especially when joined with bold exploration of the unknown. Most of our mountains are of rounded shape, and though climbing them is often hard work, it is rarely difficult or dangerous, save in bad weather, or after a snowfall. But there are many of which this is not true; the Tetons, for instance, and various glacier-bearing peaks in the Northwest; while the lofty, snow-clad ranges of British Columbia and Alaska offer one of the finest fields in the world for the daring cragsman. Mountaineering is among the manliest of sports; and it is to be hoped that some of our young men with a taste for hard work and adventure among the high hills will attempt the conquest of these great untrodden mountains of their own continent. As with all pioneer work, there would be far more discomfort and danger, far more need to display resolution, hardihood, and wisdom in such an attempt than in any expedition on well known and historic ground like the Swiss Alps; but the victory would be a hundred-fold better worth winning.

The dweller or sojourner in the wilderness who most keenly loves and appreciates his wild surroundings, and all their sights and sounds, is the man who also loves and appreciates the books which tell of them.

Foremost of all American writers on outdoor life is John Burroughs; and I can scarcely suppose that any man who cares for existence outside the cities

would willingly be without anything that he has
ever written. To the naturalist, to the observer and
lover of nature, he is of course worth many times
more than any closet systematist; and though he has
not been very much in really wild regions, his
pages so thrill with the sights and sounds of
outdoor life that nothing by any writer who is a
mere professional scientist or a mere professional
hunter can take their place, or do more than
supplement them—for scientist and hunter alike
would do well to remember that before a book can
take the highest rank in any particular line it must
also rank high in literature proper. Of course, for
us Americans, Burroughs has a peculiar charm that
he cannot have for others, no matter how much they,
too, may like him; for what he writes of is our own,
and he calls to our minds memories and associations
that are very dear. His books make us homesick
when we read them in foreign lands; for they
spring from our soil as truly as *Snowbound* or
*The Biglow Papers.**

As a woodland writer, Thoreau comes second only
to Burroughs.

For natural history in the narrower sense there are
still no better books than Audubon and Bachman's
Mammals and Audubon's Birds. There are also
good works by men like Coues and Bendire; and if
Hart Merriam, of the Smithsonian, will only do
for the mammals of the United States what he has
already done for those of the Adirondacks, we shall
have the best book of its kind in existence. Nor,

among less technical writings, should one overlook such essays as those of Maurice Thompson and Olive Thorne Miller.

There have been many American hunting-books; but too often they have been very worthless, even when the writers possessed the necessary first-hand knowledge, and the rare capacity of seeing the truth. Few of the old-time hunters ever tried to write of what they had seen and done; and of those who made the effort fewer still succeeded. Innate refinement and the literary faculty—that is, the faculty of writing a thoroughly interesting and readable book, full of valuable information—may exist in uneducated people; but if they do not, no amount of experience in the field can supply their lack. However, we have had some good works on the chase and habits of big game, such as Caton's *Deer and Antelope of America*, Van Dyke's *Still-Hunter*, Elliott's *Carolina Sports*, and Dodge's *Hunting Grounds of the Great West*, besides the Century Company's *Sport with Rod and Gun*. Then there is Catlin's book, and the journals of the explorers from Lewis and Clark down; and occasional volumes on outdoor life, such as Theodore Winthrop's *Canoe and Saddle*, and Clarence King's *Mountaineering in the Sierra Nevada*.

Two or three of the great writers of American literature, notably Parkman in his *Oregon Trail* and, with less interest, Irving in his *Trip on the Prairies* have written with power and charm of life in the American wilderness; but no one has arisen to do for the far western plainsmen and Rocky Mountain trappers quite what Herman Melville did for the South Sea whaling folk in *Omoo* and *Moby Dick*. The best description of these old-time dwellers among the mountains and on the plains is to be found in a couple of good volumes by the Englishman Ruxton. However, the backwoodsmen proper, both in their forest home and when they first began to venture out on the prairie, have been portrayed by a master hand. In a succession of wonderfully drawn characters, ranging from "Aaron Thousandacres" to "Ishmael Bush," Fenimore Cooper has preserved for always the likenesses of these stark pioneer settlers and backwoods hunters; uncouth, narrow, hard, suspicious, but with all the virile virtues of a young and masterful race, a race of mighty breeders, mighty fighters, mighty commonwealth builders. As for Leatherstocking, he is one of the undying men of story; grand, simple, kindly, pure-minded, staunchly loyal, the type of the steel-thewed and iron-willed hunter-warrior.

Turning from the men of fiction to the men of real life, it is worth noting how many of the leaders among our statesmen and soldiers have sought strength and pleasure in the chase, or in kindred vigorous pastimes. Of course field sports, or at least the wilder kinds, which entail the exercise of daring, and the endurance of toil and hardship, and which lead men afar into the forests and mountains, stand above athletic exercises; exactly as among the latter, rugged outdoor games, like football and lacrosse, are much superior to mere gymnastics and calisthenics.

With a few exceptions the men among us who have stood foremost in political leadership, like their fellows who have led our armies, have been of stalwart frame and sound bodily health. When they sprang from the frontier folk, as did Lincoln and Andrew Jackson, they usually hunted much in their youth, if only as an incident in the prolonged warfare waged by themselves and their kinsmen against the wild forces of nature. Old Israel Putnam's famous wolf-killing feat comes strictly under this head. Doubtless he greatly enjoyed the excitement of the adventure; but he went into it as a matter of business, not of sport. The wolf, the last of its kind in his neighborhood, had taken heavy toll of the flocks of himself and his friends; when they found the deep cave in which it had made its den it readily beat off the dogs sent in to assail it; and so Putnam crept in himself with his torch and his flint-lock musket, and shot the beast where it lay.

When such men lived in long settled and thickly peopled regions, they needs had to accommodate themselves to the conditions and put up with humbler forms of sport. Webster, like his great rival for Whig leadership, Henry Clay, cared much for horses, dogs, and guns; but though an outdoor man he had no chance to develop a love for big-game hunting. He was, however, very fond of the rod and shotgun. Mr. Cabot Lodge recently handed me a letter written to his grandfather by Webster, and describing a day's trout fishing. It may be worth giving for the sake of the writer, and because of the fine heartiness and zest in enjoyment which it shows:

Sandwich, June 4, Saturday Mor'g 6 O'clock
Dear Sir:
    I send you eight or nine trout, which I took yesterday, in that chief of all brooks, Mashpee. I made a long day of it, and with good success, for me. John was with me, full of good advice, but did not fish—nor carry a rod.

I took 26 trouts, all weighing	17 lb.	12 oz.
The largest (you have him) weighed at Crokers	2 lb.	4 oz.
The five largest	3 lb.	5 oz.
The eight largest	11 lb.	8 oz.

I got these by following your advice; that is, *by careful & thorough* fishing of the difficult places, which others do not fish. The brook is fished, nearly every day. I entered it, not so high up as we sometimes do, between 7 & 8 o'clock, & at 12 was hardly more than half way down to the meeting house path. You see I did not hurry. The day did not hold out to fish the whole brook properly. The largest trout I took at 3 p.m. (you see I am precise) below the meeting house, under a bush on the right bank, two or three rods below the large *beeches*. It is singular, that in the whole day, I did not take two trouts out of the same hole. I found both ends, or parts of the Brook about equally productive. Small fish not plenty, in either. So many hooks get everything which is not hid away in the manner large trouts take care of themselves. I hooked one, which I suppose to be larger than any which I took, as he broke my line, by fair pulling, after I had pulled him out of his den, & was playing him in fair open water.

Of what I send you, I pray you keep what you wish yourself, send three to Mr. Ticknor, & three to Dr. Warren; or two of the larger ones, to each will perhaps be enough—& if there be any left, there is Mr. Callender & Mr. Blake, & Mr. Davis, either of them not "averse to fish." Pray let Mr. Davis *see* them— *especially the large one.*—As he promised to come, & fell back, I desire to excite his regrets. I hope you will have the large one on your own table.

The day was fine—not another hook in the Brook. John steady as a judge—and every thing else exactly right. I never, on the whole, had so agreeable a day's fishing tho the result, in pounds or numbers, is not great;—nor ever expect such another.

Please preserve this letter but rehearse not these particulars to the uninitiated.

I think the Limerick *not* the best hook. Whether it pricks too soon, or for what other reason, I found, or thought I found, the fish more likely to let go his hold, from this, than from the old fashioned hook.

Yrs., D. Webster (H. Cabot, Esq.)

The greatest of Americans, Washington, was very fond of hunting, both with rifle or fowling-piece, and especially with horse, horn, and hound. Essentially the representative of all that is best in our national life, standing high as a general, high as a statesman, and highest of all as a man, he could never have been what he was had he not taken delight in feats of hardihood, of daring, and of bodily prowess. He was strongly drawn to those field sports which demand in their follower the exercise of the manly virtues—courage, endurance, physical address. As a young man, clad in the distinctive garb of the backwoodsman, the fringed and tasselled hunting-shirt, he led the life of a frontier surveyor; and like his fellow adventurers in wilderness exploration and Indian campaigning, he was often forced to trust to the long rifle for keeping his party in food. When at his home, at Mount Vernon, he hunted from simple delight in the sport.

His manuscript diaries, preserved in the State Department at Washington, are full of entries concerning his feats in the chase; almost all of them naturally falling in the years between the ending of the French war and the opening of the Revolutionary struggle against the British, or else in the period separating his service as Commander-in-chief of the Continental armies from his term of office as President of the Republic. These entries are scattered through others dealing with his daily duties in overseeing his farm and mill, his attendance at the Virginia House of Burgesses, his journeys, the drill of the local militia, and all the various interests of his many-sided life. Fond though he was of hunting, he was wholly incapable of the career of inanity led by those who make sport, not a manly pastime, but the one serious business of their lives.

The entries in the diaries are short, and are couched in the homely vigorous English, so familiar to the readers of Washington's journals and private letters. Sometimes they are brief jottings in reference to shooting trips; such as: "Rid out with my gun"; "went pheasant hunting"; "went ducking," and "went a gunning up the Creek." But far more often they are: "Rid out with my hounds," "Went a fox hunting," or "went a hunting." In their perfect simplicity and good faith they are strongly characteristic of the man. He enters his blank days and failures as conscientiously as his red-letter days of success; recording with equal care on one day, "Fox hunting with Captain Posey—catch a Fox," and another, "Went a hunting with Lord Fairfax... catched nothing."

Occasionally he began as early as August and continued until April; and while he sometimes made but eight or ten hunts in a season, at others he made as many in a month. Often he hunted from Mt. Vernon, going out once or twice a week, either alone or with a party of his friends and neighbors; and again he would meet with these same neighbors at one of their houses, and devote several days solely to the chase. The country was still very wild, and now and then game was encountered with which the fox-hounds proved unable to cope; as witness entries like: "found both a Bear and a Fox, but got neither"; "Went a hunting... started a Deer & then a Fox but got neither"; and "Went a hunting and after trailing a fox a good while the Dogs Raized a Deer & ran out of the Neck with it & did not some of them at least come home till the next day." If it was a small animal, however, it was soon accounted for. "Went a Hunting...catched a Rakoon but never found a Fox."

The woods were so dense and continuous that it was often impossible for the riders to keep close to the hounds throughout the run; though in one or two of the best covers, as the journal records, Washington "directed paths to be cut for Fox Hunting." This thickness of the timber made it difficult to keep the hounds always under control; and there are frequent allusions to their going off on their own account, as "Joined some dogs that were self hunting." Sometimes the hounds got so far away that it was impossible to tell whether they had killed or not, the journal remarking "catched nothing that we know of," or "found a fox at the head of the blind Pocoson which we suppose was killed in an hour but could not find it."

Another result of this density and continuity of cover was the frequent recurrence of days of ill success. There are many such entries as: "Went Fox hunting, but started nothing"; "Went a hunting, but catched nothing"; "found nothing"; "found a Fox and lost it." Often failure followed long and hard runs: "Started a Fox, run him four hours, took the Hounds off at night"; "found a Fox and run it 6 hours and then lost"; "Went a hunting above Darrells...found a fox by two Dogs but lost it upon joining the Pack." In the season of 1772-73 Washington hunted eighteen days and killed nine foxes; and though there were seasons when he was out much more often, this proportion of kills to runs was if anything above the average. At the beginning of 1768 he met with a series of blank days which might well have daunted a less patient and persevering hunter. In January and the early part of February he was out nine times without getting a thing; but his diary does not contain a word of disappointment or surprise, each successive piece of ill-luck being entered without comment, even when one day he met some more fortunate friends "who had just catched 2 foxes." At last, on February 12th, he himself "catched two foxes"; the six or eight gentlemen of the neighborhood who made up the field all went home with him to Mt. Vernon, to dine and pass the night, and in the hunt of the following day they repeated the feat of a double score. In the next seven days' hunting he killed four times.

The runs of course varied greatly in length; on one day he "found a bitch fox at Piney Branch and killed it in an hour"; on another he "killed a Dog fox after having him on foot three hours & hard running an hour and a qr."; and on yet another he "catched a fox with a bobd Tail & cut ears after 7 hours chase in which most of the Dogs were worsted." Sometimes he caught his fox in thirty-five minutes, and again he might run it nearly the whole day in vain; the average run seems to have been from an hour and a half to three hours. Sometimes the entry records merely the barren fact of the run; at others a few particulars are given, with homespun, telling directness, as: "Went a hunting with Jacky Custis and catched a Bitch Fox after three hours chase—founded it on ye. ck. by I.

Soals"; or "went a Fox hunting with Lund Washington—took the drag of a fox by Isaac Gates & carrd. it tolerably well to the old Glebe then touched now and then upon a cold scent till we came into Col. Fairfaxes Neck where we found about half after three upon the Hills just above Accotinck Creek—after running till quite Dark took off the Dogs and came home."

The foxes were doubtless mostly of the gray kind, and besides going to holes they treed readily. In January, 1770, he was out seven days, killing four foxes; and two of the entries in the journal relate to foxes which treed; one, on the 10th, being, "I went a hunting in the Neck and visited the plantn. there found and killed a bitch fox after treeing it 3 t. chasg. it abt. 3 hrs.," and the other, on the 23rd: "Went a hunting after breakfast & found a Fox at muddy hole & killed her (it being a bitch) after a chase of better than two hours and after treeing her twice the last of which times she fell dead out of the Tree after being therein sevl. minutes apparently." In April, 1769, he hunted four days, and on every occasion the fox treed. April 7th, "Dog fox killed, ran an hour & treed twice." April 11th, "Went a fox hunting and took a fox alive after running him to a Tree—brot him home." April 12th, "Chased the above fox an hour & 45 minutes when he treed again after which we lost him." April 13th, "Killed a dog fox after treeing him in 35 minutes."

Washington continued his fox-hunting until, in the spring of 1775, the guns of the minute-men in Massachusetts called him to the command of the

Revolutionary soldiery. When the eight weary
years of campaigning were over, he said good-by to
the war-worn veterans whom he had led through
defeat and disaster to ultimate triumph, and
became once more a Virginia country gentleman.
Then he took up his fox-hunting with as much zest
as ever. The entries in his journal are now rather
longer, and go more into detail than formerly.
Thus, on December 12th, 1785, he writes that after
an early breakfast he went on a hunt and found a fox
at half after ten, "being first plagued with the dogs
running hogs," followed on his drag for some time,
then ran him hard for an hour, when there came a
fault; but when four dogs which had been thrown
out rejoined the pack they put the fox up afresh,
and after fifty minutes' run killed him in an open
field, "every Rider & every Dog being present at
the Death." With his usual alternations between
days like this, and days of ill-luck, he hunted
steadily every season until his term of private life
again drew to a close and he was called to the
headship of the nation he had so largely helped to
found.

In a certain kind of fox-hunting lore there is much
reference to a Warwickshire squire who, when the
Parliamentary and Royalist armies were forming
for the battle at Edgehill, was discovered between
the hostile lines, unmovedly drawing the covers for
a fox. Now, this placid sportsman should by rights
have been slain offhand by the first trooper who
reached him, whether Cavalier or Roundhead. He
had mistaken means for ends, he had confounded
the healthful play which should fit a man for

needful work with the work itself; and mistakes of this kind are sometimes criminal. Hardy sports of the field offer the best possible training for war; but they become contemptible when indulged in while the nation is at death-grips with her enemies.

It was not in Washington's strong nature to make such an error. Nor yet, on the other hand, was he likely to undervalue either the pleasure, or the real worth of outdoor sports. The qualities of heart, mind, and body, which made him delight in the hunting-field, and which he there exercised and developed, stood him in good stead in many a long campaign and on many a stricken field; they helped to build that stern capacity for leadership in war which he showed alike through the bitter woe of the winter at Valley Forge, on the night when he ferried his men across the half-frozen Delaware to the overthrow of the German mercenaries at Trenton, and in the brilliant feat of arms whereof the outcome was the decisive victory of Yorktown.

Footnote

* I am under many obligations to the writings of Mr. Burroughs (though there are one or two of his theories from which I should dissent); and there is a piece of indebtedness in this very volume of which I have only just become aware. In my chapter on the prong-buck there is a paragraph which will at once suggest to any lover of Burroughs some sentences in his essay on "Birds and Poets." I did not notice the resemblance until happening to reread the essay after my own chapter was written, and at the time I had no idea that I was borrowing from anybody, the more so as I was thinking purely of western wilderness life and western wilderness game, with which I knew Mr. Burroughs had never been familiar. I have concluded to leave the paragraph in with this acknowledgment.

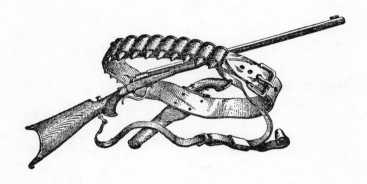

Memories of the American Frontier

In this volume I have avoided repeating what was contained in either of my former books, the *Hunting Trips of a Ranchman* and *Ranch Life and the Hunting Trail*. For many details of life and work in the cattle country I must refer the reader to these two volumes; and also for more full accounts of the habits and methods of hunting such game as deer and antelope. As far as I know, the description in my *Ranch Life* of the habits and the chase of the mountain sheep is the only moderately complete account thereof that has ever been published.

There have been many changes, both in my old hunting-grounds and my old hunting-friends, since I first followed the chase in the far western country. Where the buffalo and the Indian ranged, along the Little Missouri, the branded herds of the ranchmen now graze; the scene of my elk-hunt at Two Ocean Pass is now part of the National Forest Reserve; settlers and miners have invaded the ground where I killed bear and moose; and steamers ply on the lonely water of Kootenai Lake.

Of my hunting companions some are alive;
others—among them my staunch and valued
friend, Will Dow, and crabbed, surly old Hank
Griffen—are dead; while yet others have drifted
away, and I know not what has become of them.

I have made no effort to indicate the best kind of
camp kit for hunting, for the excellent reason that it
depends so much upon the kind of trip taken, and
upon the circumstances of the person taking it. The
hunting trip may be made with a pack-train, or
with a wagon, or with a canoe, or on foot; and the
hunter may have half a dozen attendants, or he may
go absolutely alone. I have myself made trips under
all of these circumstances. At times I have gone
with two or three men, several tents, and an
elaborate apparatus for cooking, cases of canned
goods, and the like. On the other hand, I have
made trips on horseback, with nothing whatsoever
beyond what I had on, save my oil-skin slicker,
a metal cup, and some hardtack, tea, and salt in
the saddle pockets; and I have gone for a week or
two's journey on foot, carrying on my shoulders
my blanket, a frying-pan, some salt, a little flour,
a small chunk of bacon, and a hatchet. So it is with
dress. The clothes should be stout, of a neutral
tint; the hat should be soft, without too large a
brim; the shoes heavy, and the soles studded with
small nails, save when moccasins or rubber-soled
shoes are worn; but within these limits there is
room for plenty of variation. Avoid, however,
the so-called deer-stalker's cap, which is an
abomination; its peaked brim giving no protection
whatsoever to the eyes when facing the sun

quartering, a position in which many shots must be taken. In very cold regions, fur coats, caps, and mittens, and all-wool underclothing are necessary. I dislike rubber boots when they can possibly be avoided. In hunting in snow in the winter I use the so-called German socks and felt overshoes where possible. One winter I had an ermine cap made. It was very good for peeping over the snowy ridge crests when game was on the other side; but, except when the entire landscape was snow-covered, it was an unmitigated nuisance. In winter, webbed snow-shoes are used in the thick woods, and skees in the open country.

There is an endless variety of opinion about rifles, and all that can be said with certainty is that any good modern rifle will do. It is the man behind the rifle that counts, after the weapon has reached a certain stage of perfection. One of my friends invariably uses an old Government Springfield, a 45-calibre, with an ounce bullet. Another cares for nothing but the 40-90 Sharps', a weapon for which I myself have much partiality. Another uses always the old 45-calibre Sharps', and yet another the 45-calibre Remington. Two of the best bear and elk hunters I know prefer the 32- and 38-calibre Marlin's, with long cartridges, weapons with which I myself would not undertake to produce any good results. Yet others prefer pieces of very large calibre. The amount of it is that each one of these guns possesses some excellence which the others lack, but which is in most cases atoned for by some corresponding defect. Simplicity of mechanism is very important, but so is rapidity of fire; and it is hard to get both of them developed to the highest degree in the same piece. In the same way, flatness of trajectory, penetration, range, shock, and accuracy are all qualities which must be attained; but to get one in perfection usually means the sacrifice of some of the rest. For instance, other things being equal, the smallest calibre has the greatest penetration, but gives the least shock; while a very flat trajectory, if acquired by heavy charges of powder, means the sacrifice of accuracy. Similarly, solid and hollow pointed bullets have, respectively, their merits and demerits. There is no use of dogmatizing about weapons. Some which prove excellent for particular countries and kinds of hunting are useless in others.

There seems to be no doubt, judging from the testimony of sportsmen in South Africa and in India, that very heavy calibre double-barrelled rifles are best for use in the dense jungles and against the thick-hided game of those regions; but they are of very little value with us. In 1882 one of the buffalo hunters on the Little Missouri obtained from some Englishman a double-barrelled ten-bore rifle of the kind used against rhinoceros, buffalo, and elephant in the Old World; but it proved very inferior to the 40- and 45-calibre Sharps' buffalo guns when used under the conditions of American buffalo hunting, the tremendous shock given by the bullet not compensating for the gun's great relative deficiency in range and accuracy, while even the penetration was inferior at ordinary distances. It is largely also a matter of individual taste. At one time I possessed a

very expensive double-barrelled 500 Express, by
one of the crack English makers; but I never liked
the gun, and could not do as well with it as with my
repeater, which cost barely a sixth as much. So one
day I handed it to a Scotch friend, who was
manifestly ill at ease with a Winchester exactly like
my own. He took to the double-barrel as naturally
as I did to the repeater, and did excellent work
with it. Personally, I have always preferred the
Winchester. I now use a 45-90, with my old buffalo
gun, a 40-90 Sharps, as spare rifle. Both,
of course, have specially tested barrels, and are
stocked and sighted to suit myself.

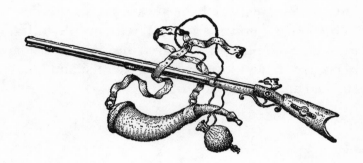